MARQUETRY
TECHNIQUES

MARQUETRY TECHNIQUES

DAVID MIDDLETON
and
ALAN TOWNSEND

B. T. Batsford • London

First published 1993
© David Middleton and Alan Townsend, 1993

Typeset by Goodfellow & Egan, Cambridge
and printed in Great Britain by The Bath Press, Avon

Published by
B.T. Batsford Ltd
4 Fitzhardinge Street
London W1H 0AH

A catalogue record for this book is available from the British Library

ISBN 0 7134 6986 2

ACKNOWLEDGEMENTS

To Marion and Anne, our wives, for showing enormous patience and understanding.

To Doug Crome, for his expertise with the camera in producing the colour photographs.

To various members of the Chelmsford Marquetry Group, for permission to photograph and publish some of their items of applied marquetry.

And finally to the Marquetry Society of Great Britain, without whom we would never have developed our skills to their present level.

CONTENTS

The Old Mexican Church, whose construction is described, step by step, in Chapter 8.

INTRODUCTION

Wood is one of the oldest natural materials which has survived into our modern synthetic age. Its warmth and beauty have never successfully been imitated. Now, hundreds of exotic hardwood timbers and veneers are readily available and these, put into the hands of the cabinet-maker/marquetarian, can be used to create articles of enduring beauty. Fortunately our hardwood forests are a renewable resource and good programmed management will ensure us a constant, though somewhat limited, supply over the years to come.

From the sixteenth century the French, Dutch, and later the English used marquetry and parquetry to decorate furniture as well as Buhl works which incorporated brass and mother-of-pearl. Many pieces have survived the ravages of time and can now be seen in stately homes and museums across the world. Veneers for these craftsman were saw cut and about 3 mm ($^{1}/_{8}$in.) thick, which made the cutting of intricate pieces very difficult. This cutting was done with a saw donkey, a large foot- or power-driven fret saw. The modern marquetarian's job is much easier as veneers are now thinly sliced, about 0.9–0.6 mm ($^{1}/_{28}$–$^{1}/_{40}$ in.) thick, so that it is possible to cut them with a craft knife or scalpel.

The aim of this book is to provide an insight to the beginner into the world of applied marquetry and some of its techniques as well as teaching basic marquetry methods. (We cannot teach the skills; it is up to you to acquire them by practice.) It is also intended to provide the experienced practitioner with ideas and expert advice and the craftsman/cabinet-maker with the opportunity to decorate his or her furniture and other items with designs or pictures made up of fine veneers.

In Part 1 we explain modern marquetry techniques in detail and take you through making a picture, step by step; in Part 2 we show how these techniques can be applied to a range of small and larger items; and in the Appendix we give basic outline plans for a selection of designs, to help get you started.

Our combined credentials include many years in the veneer-preparing and cabinet-making trades plus years of marquetry experience. As well as many prizes in marquetry exhibitions and showing our work as far away as Japan, we have managed to win the Marquetry Society of Great Britain's premier award, the 'Rose Bowl', four times between us (three of those by Alan) in a five-year period. We are currently passing on our thoughts, knowledge and experience every week to the members of the very successful Chelmsford Marquetry Group (the winners of the Marquetry Society's 'Group Shield' for six years running). We feel our knowledge and experience can also help you and hope you enjoy this book and your journey into marquetry.

Alan Townsend and David Middleton

PART

1

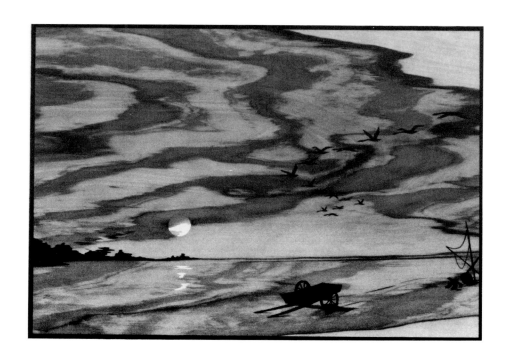

Basic Materials, Tools and Equipment

This section includes all the items necessary to produce a range of marquetry and parquetry subjects set on a flat sheet with square edges. Some of the more expensive items can be borrowed and it may be that a friend or friendly store keeper can do some of the basic woodwork or mounting for you. Basic marquetry need not be expensive, especially if you avoid the more elaborate applied pieces which require specialist woodworking tools. Detailed instructions on the use of individual pieces of equipment may be found in later chapters where appropriate.

VENEERS

A veneer is 'a thin layer of wood, marble, ivory etc. glued to a surface over another material or materials of inferior quality'. In marquetry we use only wood veneers which are purchased ready cut to a standard thickness (though unfortunately there is more than one standard!). These can be purchased from specialist suppliers and from craft shops who usually have a limited range of small pieces. Woodwork exhibitions often have the best range of veneers available under a single roof and also give the opportunity to see a little of the range and quality available through the mail order dealers. The price of veneers varies depending on rarity, availability (not necessarily the same thing), size of sheet, quality of figuring and the supplier (what is rare for one may be commonplace for another). The best veneers for marquetry may not always be the most expensive!

In any one picture, particularly a basic picture, or a parquetry design, you are unlikely to require more than about 10 to 15 veneers. As initial stock choose as far as possible those which are easier to cut as well

as a good tone range. The following list may help as a guide (most are in the colour section):

Olive ash
Aspen
Castella
Horse chestnut
Harewood
    (dark and light)
Magnolia
Pear
Rio rosewood
Sapele–crown cut
Sycamore
European walnut
    (sapwood and heartwood)
Yew

KNIFE (Fig. 1)

The most important item of equipment, but the most difficult to give advice on, is the craft knife. A range of suitable knives is available, but what suits one person may not suit another.

The basic variations are in shape (round and flat) and in the material (metal or plastic) of the handle. The method of clamping the blade can sometimes create a problem, for instance the small knurled screw on the side of one type can, after a relatively short time, rub the second finger sore. Many marquetarians prefer a little weight in the knife and hence prefer a metal handle, some adding extra weight and better grip as home-made optional extras.

The brass Swan Morton scalpel handle no. 3 is widely used. Its flat shape and deep grooved sides give good potential for control, but the blade is

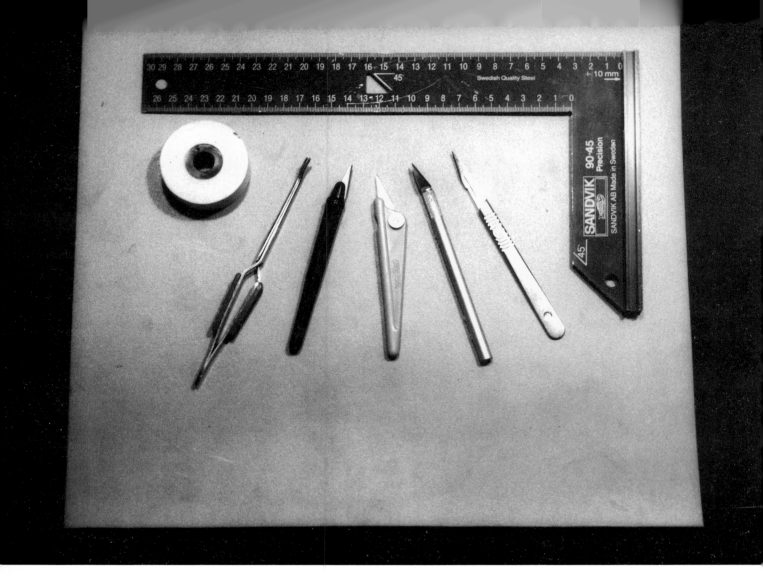

Fig. 1 Basic tools - four knives fitted with suitable blades,
tweezers for sand shading and masking tape, on a vinyl tile used
as a cheap cutting mat

flexible and needs extra support from the second finger. The blades fit into a grooved projection which locates the slot cut into the blade, the elasticity of the blade locking it in place. Another problem with this knife is that the blade can be difficult to remove.

The round metal craft knives have a knurled collar giving a good grip and the ability to twist the knife during cutting, a practice which could be expensive on blades for the beginner.

A round plastic marquetry knife is also available, in which a taper collet action clamps the blade in any position. It accepts a range of manufacturers' blades. Its rather bulbous head can obscure the blade tip but many marquetarions find it an excellent cutting tool.

The blade is of course the most important part of the knife. Unfortunately, the various requirements of the ideal blade are not compatible with the materials available. The ideal blade would have a sharp point and cutting edge, be very thin and very stiff, hard

and tough. However, the stiffness can only be obtained by a thick blade and hence the thinnest blades tend to be too flexible. To produce a blade which has reasonable stiffness but is also very thin at the cutting tip, a little modification with a carborundum stone is required. After all, craft knives are not in the main specifically designed for marquetry and the Swan Morton tool is basically a scalpel. The tip of the tool only is thinned down as shown in figs. 2–4 and further described in Chapter 6 under Fine tooth cutting.

CUTTING BOARD

You can use a piece of thick cardboard but it will not last long. Deep scoring of the cardboard can pull the knife into a previously cut line as you work, and also cutting into the abrasive card will shorten the life of your knife blades.

A tile, 400 × 300 mm (8 × 12 in.) of industrial vinyl

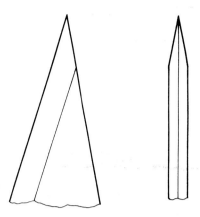

Fig. 2 Cutting point as supplied

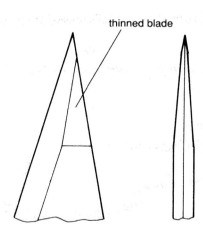

thinned blade

Fig. 3 Cutting point modified to thin blade

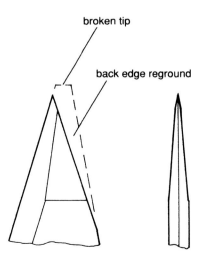

broken tip

back edge reground

Fig. 4 Cutting resharpened on back edge to remove the broken point and thinned again

floor covering makes a good cutting mat. An excellent cutting board can also be made from draughting sheet, a thin pale green vinyl-based material used for drawing-board surfaces. You glue this, with contact adhesive, to both sides of a piece of five-ply plywood.

There are also commercial cutting mats (Fig.1), which are excellent products and well worth the investment for the committed marquetarian. These are of A2 or A3 size with a self-healing surface.

STEEL RULE AND STRAIGHT EDGE

For accurate measurement you cannot beat a good quality engineer's rule 300 mm (12 in.) long. A 0.6 m (24 in.) or 1 m (36 in.) steel rule is handy for larger pieces of work. The steel rule can also double as a straight edge at a pinch but its lack of stiffness and the smooth faces can make it difficult to hold firm and prevent slipping when you are cutting long straight edges. The lack of thickness also makes it possible for the knife to ride up over the edge, resulting in shorter fingers and stained veneers!

A formed steel rule is one popular method of overcoming these two problems, the raised groove down the centre protecting the fingers, and the angled sides biting into the veneer to give greater grip. Fig. 5 shows a typical cross-section. However, the cutting edge is not very smooth, due to the deep cut graduations, and blades can take a terrible battering. A better alternative is a strip of mild, or preferably stainless, steel, 3–6 mm ($\frac{1}{8}$–$\frac{1}{4}$ in.) thick and 40–50 mm ($1\frac{1}{2}$–2 in.) wide by about 400 mm (16 in.) long.

VENEER TAPE (Fig. 1)

This is thin white paper with a gummed backing used in the trade to hold sheets of veneer together edge to edge. For its thickness it is remarkably strong and the damp tape, after a good lick, expands

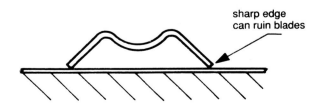

sharp edge can ruin blades

Fig. 5 Section through formed steel rule

slightly. On drying, which takes only a few minutes, it contracts again, drawing the edges firmly together. This tape should be used sparingly. Only long edges need to be taped. Most small pieces put in by the window method will hold in place by the glued edges without the assistance of tape. Moreover, several layers of tape can present a major resistance to cutting, the thin tape and gum forming an extremely tough mat when laminated.

All tape should be applied to the face side of the veneers; it can remain in place until after it has been applied to its mounting board, and can then be removed with safety with abrasive paper or a cabinet scraper.

Some books recommend that the whole of the prepared veneer should have the face side covered in veneer tape. We would strongly advise against this practice; it can mean a considerable amount of hard work when it comes to removing the tape. Removing the tape from the veneer before mounting is also to be discouraged; it is so easy at this stage to damage the veneer. Easing the problem of tape removal by damping the surface can, if not done with considerable care, result in the production of a veneer jigsaw puzzle.

SELF-ADHESIVE TAPE

This is useful for temporary fixing between veneers when marking through the window on to your selected veneer. Being tougher than veneer tape it also makes a very good hinge between tracing paper and subject, and tracing paper and waster veneer.

The best tape to use is draughting tape which has limited adhesion and hence can be removed with relative ease, although, because of the porosity of the wood, adhesion is often proportional with time as the adhesive hardens.

Don't use one of the clear tapes as these have an adhesive which is more penetrating and likely to remain in the fibres of the wood when the plastic strip is removed. These deposits can be very difficult to clean off and may result in problems in the subsequent polishing operation. When you remove the more persistent type of tape you may also pull out some of the surface fibres of the wood, forming voids which must be sanded out, a very laborious business, or filled with the finishing media, a process to be avoided if possible.

Masking tape is a readily available and relatively cheap product which is similar to draught tape but with slightly greater adhesion; it is a reasonable alternative.

ADHESIVES

Adhesives are required to glue the veneer into the waster sheet edge-to-edge, and to glue the sheet of veneer or completed marquetry to the mounting board. The first operation requires a PVA adhesive which is rubbed into the joints of the veneers after they are assembled. For the second, you can use a PVA adhesive, a contact adhesive, a two part thermo-setting (e.g. Beetle) adhesive, Cascamite, or a glue film.

A contact adhesive is the easiest to use if you don't have access to a press; details of the methods used for the various adhesives are given in Chapter 7.

A 'RUBBER' (Fig. 6)

This is a small piece of rectangular hardwood radiused off at one end, and can easily be made with the simplest of tools. It is used to 'rub' down the joints between veneers after the PVA adhesive has been applied, to ensure the surface is level at the joint.

ROLLER

You will need a roller if you are going to use contact adhesive to glue the veneers to the mounting board. It is a small wooden, or preferably hard rubber, roller about 25–30 mm in diameter (1–1^{1}/4 in.) by about 50 mm (2 in.) long with a small handle and is commonly sold as a wallpapering aid. It is used to ensure good contact after the adhesive is applied and the veneer and board are placed together.

PENS AND PENCILS (Fig. 6)

A good quality hard pencil, say 4H, can be sharpened to a suitable point and can do a satisfactory job, but the modern draughting pencil has the advantage of having a constant width drawing-point achieved by the very fine lead fed through a tube. Apart from the constant width line and no sharpening, the main advantage is the fact that a softer lead can be used and hence a denser line produced.

For tracing a design a draughting pen is ideal. These also work using a fine tube, but this time the outside of the tube is the diameter specified and the width of the line drawn. A fine wire through the centre of the tube controls the flow of ink, which is usually black waterproof ink as used by draughtsmen. Here again the line width is constant, is dense, is virtually permanent and can be very fine, typically 0.3 mm in diameter.

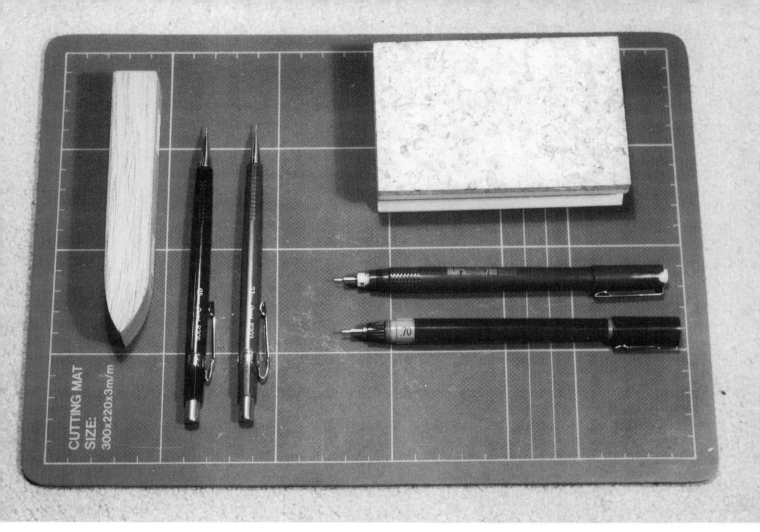

Fig. 6 Draughting pencils and pens, 'rubber' and sanding block, on a commercial cutting mat

For just marking through from your design to the veneer using carbon paper it is possible to use a stylus with a small radius (rather than a point) on the end. This is similar to a very hard pencil and has the same problems, which include the possibility of cutting through the paper and being unable to see from the face the lines which have been traced.

TRACING PAPER

You will need tracing paper to transfer your chosen design from the source material to the waster. A3 paper is a good size to have available, of weight (thickness) between 60 and 90 gsm. It is also the ideal material on which to create your marquetry and parquetry designs as it is relatively tough and both pencil and ink can be erased from its surface.

CARBON PAPER

Black carbon is the standard colour to use as most wasters are light in colour, but red also works well and yellow is useful if you are working on a dark

waster. Never use a blue carbon. For some reason the colour gives a permanent stain which is likely to get transferred to the face side of the veneer.

MOUNTING BOARD

To begin with chipboard should do, 12 mm (^{1}/2 in.) thick for a small picture and 15 mm (^{5}/8 in.) for anything over about 200 mm (8 in.) square.

Medium-density fibreboard (MDF) is a better quality material and should be considered as your standard of work improves. Many small shops will cut your board accurately to size and with a suitably finished square edge.

ABRASIVE PAPER

Silicon carbide papers in grades 150 and 240 are the most suitable for rubbing down the surface of the veneer after it has been mounted while 240 and 320 grades are used for flatting the surface after the polish has been applied. Wet-and-dry is ideal to start the polishing process by reducing the scratch size and a 600 grade would be adequate.

SANDING BLOCK (Fig. 6)

Simply a flat backing block for the abrasive paper, this can be purchased as a solid block of cork, but is simple to make using a piece of wood with a cork tile as a facing. This home-made version tends to be slightly harder, longer lasting and can be made a little larger than the commercial cork blocks.

POLISHING MATERIAL

Details of polishes are given in Chapter 7, but in general you should find cellulose sanding sealer satisfactory. It does have a strong smell, but it is not too unpleasant, and it should be used in a relatively warm, dry, dust-free and well-ventilated environment.

BURNISHING CREAM

When the polish is rubbed down flat it has a dull appearance because of the scratches on the surface you are left with, even with the finest wet-and-dry abrasive paper. To bring to a gloss finish the surface is polished with a burnishing cream. There are several specialist products that work very well, but a car colour restorer is ideal; it is readily available and not expensive.

WIRE WOOL

If you want a sheen rather than a gloss finish you need a 0000 grade of wire wool.

Further Useful Items

Here we list a few items you will find are necessary if you become more proficient with your marquetry and wish to advance to more complex work, or carry out more of the woodwork stages yourself. Again many of the items are tools already in the possession of the handyman and this hobby simply extends their potential use.

HEATER AND SAND TRAY (Fig. 7)

The purpose of the heater is to bring a tray of sand to a temperature suitable for sand shading (see Chapter 5). The sand used can be any clean, fine grit, for instance the sand sold for the floor of birdcages. Never use builder's sand; it will stain the veneer.

The tray should be sufficiently large in diameter to cover the heating element, and only about 25 mm (1 in.) deep. An old baking tray will do, but these are

a little thin and tend to corrode rather quickly. A much better alternative would be an old stainless-steel shallow serving dish or the bottom of an old aluminium or stainless steel saucepan. It is important that the tray covers the element if you use an electric heater: this will not only be much more efficient and you will be less likely to get your hands uncomfortably hot and even burn your fingers, but it will also make the element last longer as the outer ring will burn out sooner if left on a high setting and unused.

The safest and most convenient heater to use is a single-ring electrical heater. These are square and low and therefore difficult to upset, and they also have a simple temperature control.

Using a single ring on an electric or gas cooker is a short-term solution until you are convinced that you need this process.

A small gas camping-stove is another alternative but we would not recommend this because of the inherent danger they present. Only if you have an outside workshop could we advise this type of heater, and only then if it were secured to prevent it being knocked over.

TWEEZERS (see Fig. 1, p. 14)

An essential item for sand shading. Long nose pliers are a suitable alternative and keep the fingers just a little further away from the heater and hot sand. The best tweezers are those which are held closed by the spring action, eliminating the need to clamp the tweezers with your fingers all the time and giving less

Fig. 7 Sand tray on a suitable electric heater

chance of you dropping your painstakingly cut piece of veneer into the hot sand to be incinerated before it can be recovered.

ELECTRIC IRON

The iron is used to lay veneers, specifically edge veneers, using gluefilm, a thermo-setting adhesive. Any glue getting on to its surface should be cleaned off afterwards with wet-and-dry abrasive paper and then with a surface cleaner.

TRY-SQUARE

For this type of work it is important to have a try-square with a large blade to ensure that both mounting board and veneers are cut as square as possible.

LAMP

The very fine cutting required in marquetry demands a high light intensity. A counterpoise lamp is ideal.

MAGNIFIER

A number of magnifiers are available on stands of which the counterpoise type is the most manoeuvrable. Some of these magnifiers also incorporate a lamp.

PRESS (Fig. 8)

Those new to marquetry will get by using contact adhesive for mounting veneers, and many experienced marquetarians use nothing else. However, there are problems associated with contact

Fig. 8 Homemade press which has proved to be very satisfactory in use

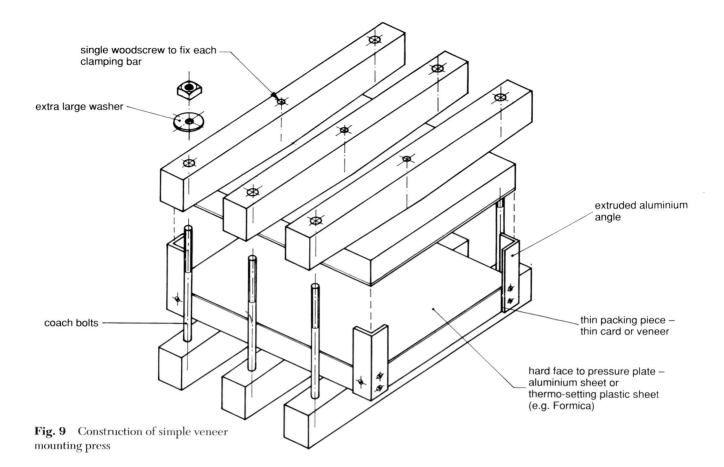

single woodscrew to fix each clamping bar

extra large washer

extruded aluminium angle

coach bolts

thin packing piece – thin card or veneer

hard face to pressure plate – aluminium sheet or thermo-setting plastic sheet (e.g. Formica)

Fig. 9 Construction of simple veneer mounting press

adhesives (discussed in Chapter 7) and you may find that you do require access to a press before long.

Old cast-iron bookbinder's presses are sometimes available, but even a relatively small press with a pressure plate about 250 by 300 mm (10 × 12 in.) is very heavy and a larger size would be impractical for anyone without a purpose-built workshop with a very solid bench and some means of transport and lifting for heavy equipment. You may be lucky to have access to a professional press who will mount your veneers for a small charge, or for a fee will let you use their heated press. Using a thermo-setting adhesive, the time taken to complete the mounting process can be reduced to a few minutes.

There are some presses on the market, but these can only be a viable proposition for a club or the really dedicated and well-off amateur. A steel version similar in construction to the bookbinder's press, but very much lighter, is available at a reasonable price, but is still limited in size. A larger area, more suitable for furniture panels, can be dealt with using a Bag press. This uses a large inflatable rubber bag which is blown up like a balloon. When this is trapped between two flat surfaces it can apply a very

large force with relatively low pressure which is uniform over the whole surface.

Or you can construct your own press, modifying the DIY press shown in Figs. 9 and 10, to produce a professional, effective and easy to use piece of equipment. The drawings give most of the information you need, but some explanation may be helpful. The dimensions may be modified to suit the size of press you require, but be careful as doubling the pressure plate size does not mean a straight doubling of all dimensions. The pressure plates can remain the same thickness, but more clamping straps will be required and they will need to be deeper to give the same stiffness over the greater length.

The main objective of any press is to maintain a perfectly flat surface when the pressure is applied. Wood is a relatively flexible material when under a bending stress, even when over 40 mm (1 $\frac{1}{2}$ in.) thick. The curves on the clamping faces of the clamping straps are designed to cater for the bending that occurs when the forces are applied at each end of the straps. It is difficult to give exact sizes for this curve, but the dimensions shown should prove reasonably successful.

Figure 11 shows a more exact method of obtaining this curve. The bolts are tightened and while the clamping straps are under this bending stress a straight line is drawn along the inside edge. On releasing the pressure the straps straighten and the straight lines become curves. The surface can then be shaped with a plane.

The extruded aluminium angle is used as a guide to prevent relative movement between the veneer and the mounting board while tightening up the bolts. It is quite easy to cut the pressure plate boards to the same size, and therefore to give clearance thin card or veneer can be clamped between the aluminium and the lower board to make the assembly of the press easy but without too much movement.

The nuts should be tightened in pairs which means wielding two spanners at once. To avoid the necessity of using spanners, the nuts could be replaced with large wing nuts. The manufacture of these parts may require the use of metalwork machines and hence present a problem for many marquetarians. Cast zinc handwheels are available, but these still require drilling and tapping to size.

The clamp straps should be made from a hardwood. Beech would be suitable, and the best material for the pressure plate is a double thickness of 20 mm (³/4 in.) blockboard. High density chipboard (or MDF) is also a good material, but does increase the weight.

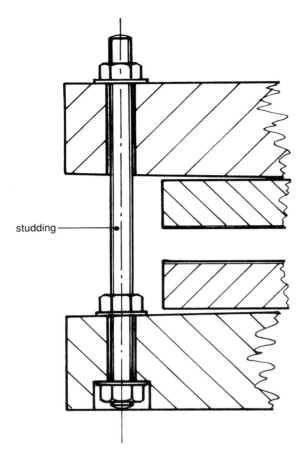

studding

Fig. 10 Easy and effective clamping for mounting press

Fig. 11 Method of determining ideal curve for faces of clamping bars.

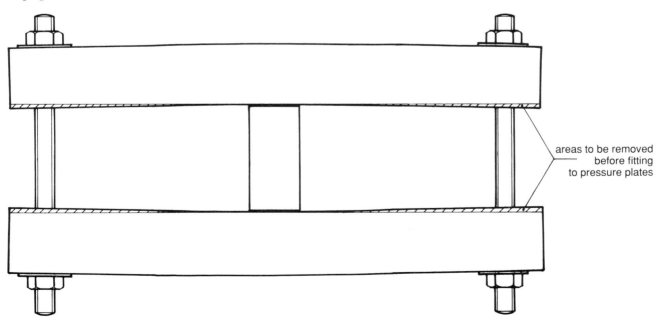

areas to be removed before fitting to pressure plates

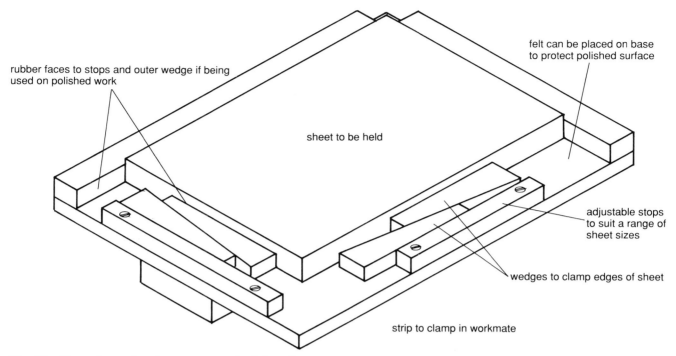

rubber faces to stops and outer wedge if being used on polished work

felt can be placed on base to protect polished surface

sheet to be held

adjustable stops to suit a range of sheet sizes

wedges to clamp edges of sheet

strip to clamp in workmate

Fig. 12   Clamp for sanding down veneer and polishing flat sheet work

The extra large washer is essential and is required to prevent excessive damage to the clamping strap. These washers are not the standard size but are available for various specialist uses.

WORKBENCH

Should you wish to do anything other than pure marquetry you may feel the need for a workbench with a vice or other devices to hold boards firm for shaping, sanding or polishing.

SANDING CLAMP

To hold flat boards steady while the face is sanded flat you need a sanding clamp. A 'workmate' can do this job but only to a limited size. The drawing in Fig. 12 shows the basic principle of a device that can be made with a very basic set of tools; the dimensions can be made to suit the largest area you think you will be attempting. The only important dimension is the depth of the retaining strips and wedges which must be thinner than the sheet to be held.

Fig. 13   Router on stand being used to produce a moulded edge on a circular picture

EXTRA EQUIPMENT FOR MORE ADVANCED MARQUETRY

ELECTRIC DRILL

This should be either a drill mounted on a stand, or even better a pillar drill.

ROUTER (Fig. 13)

A plunge router is the most versatile, and one which is mounted on a stand (like a pillar drill or underslung like a moulding machine) rather than

hand-held is better for routing small pieces. It is easier and safer to push the wood past the cutter rather than manhandle the router over the workpiece. The latter is sometimes impossible anyway, for instance with items such as small feet of the type made for the Tea Caddy (see second colour section).

The router machine can prove a costly item, but we have found the simplest of machines is as good as the most expensive for the type of work we attempt.

ROUTER CUTTERS (Fig. 14)

Cutters for routers can be rather expensive but don't fall into the trap of buying high-speed steel cutters. Tungsten-tipped cutters can cost about 50 per cent more than the H.S.S. equivalents, but their life expectancy more than makes up for this extra cost. Even when they are used on solid timber and on MDF they will have a good life, whereas H.S.S. cutters will burn out in minutes.

Much of our work uses classic shapes to reproduce the artistry that is sometimes missing in commercial items. A huge range of cutters now exists, from a wide range of companies, but only a handful will be necessary to produce a variety of mouldings.

SANDING DISC

Sanding disc machines are also available at a reasonable price. A 250 mm (10 in.) disc size is preferable. This usually comes with a protractor which is ideal for creating mitres (for the corners of jewellery boxes, etc.) very much more accurately and cleaner than with a hand saw. Also, after initial cutting with a saw, it can be used to finish sanding shapes and for making circular templates (as described in Chapter 5 using a home-made jig) to cut in inlays and stringers.

BAND SAW

A small band saw will enable you to rough cut various shapes, and circles for templates, and is essential if you wish to cut the male/female parts for the domed clock shown in Fig. 9.34 (p.00) and described in Chapter 7. A good substitute for a bandsaw is a hand-held jigsaw although this can prove somewhat limiting.

LATHE

You may feel the need for a lathe if you want to create turned pieces to decorate with marquetry or parquetry (see Chapter 7).

Fig. 14 Typical router cutters, all with tungsten carbide tips suitable for cutting MDF

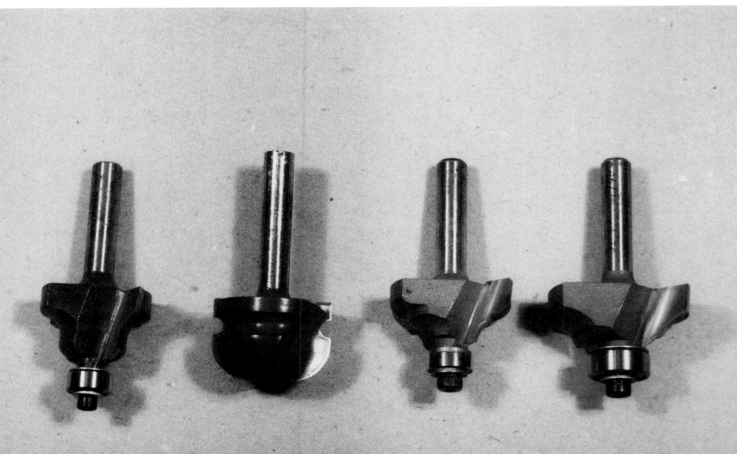

Finally, a small planer-thicknesser is useful though most wood bought at a good merchants will already be planed all square and most timber merchants, at a little extra cost, will be pleased to accommodate your specific needs. A cross-cut saw or a saw bench for a power saw with a tungsten carbide tipped blade for cutting MDF board might also come in useful, but once again a good timber merchant will cut to suit your individual needs.

SAFETY

When using any machine which throws out dust and chips, which includes all the power tools, good-quality eye protection should always be worn and if you do not own an efficient dust extraction unit (which is unlikely in most small workshops) then wear a dust mask over your mouth and nose.

Before connecting any electrical machinery check plugs and leads for damage or loose wires and before turning on machinery ensure that all guards are fitted and in the correct position. Always keep hands and fingers away from any moving parts, especially cutters, when a machine is connected to the electrical supply, even if it is not actually running.

Never take machinery for granted; large forces are at work and lack of concentration can sometimes cause tools to 'bite back'. With any power woodworking machinery good personal instruction should result in much safer working practice.

3

Veneers

THE PALETTE

Buying veneer is not like paying a visit to your local wallpaper and paint shop, where you can select your pattern and colour by a shade number. Even if you think you are familiar with the colour and nature of a species, you may find, when making a purchase, that the shade differs from the expected, the grain may not be quite the same as described, and one piece may be tough and grainy whilst the next sample will be soft and easy to work. For example, you might order holly with the reasonable expectation of receiving a perfectly white piece of veneer, only to receive through the post a pale veneer stained with wild grey markings. Similarly, you may receive sycamore with no fiddleback, or magnolia which is not very green. Take walnut, for example – it is possible with some planning to cut an entire picture using only this one wood, so diverse are the colours, grains and textures of one leaf of this wood's veneer.

We have described here over 50 veneers among those which are most popular and useful for the marquetarian. Most of them have an accompanying colour photograph, selected to give as accurate a representation of the veneer as possible.

There are about 280 to 300 species of wood available in veneer form, but very many are hard to obtain and some are of no more than curiosity value and would probably never be used, even if you could get hold of them, or afford them!

You can get by on relatively few pieces of veneer which have been wisely selected, and on average even a prize-winning picture, with the help of sand shading, will use no more than about 14 different varieties. Many of the veneers described below are shown in the first colour section or the 'Old Mexican Church' in the second colour section.

Remember, these veneers were once living material which, if you follow the appropriate methods and techniques can be preserved forever in the form of beautiful pictures or designs.

AGBA

This timber comes from West Africa. It is a light tan to straw colour and resembles some species of pale mahogany in that it has an interlocking grain, but it has much wider stripes. It also contains a resin that can appear to give it a silvery tint, but this causes no problems in cutting or finishing.

Agba is a useful alternative colour for constructing Louis cubes due to its satiny appearance. In pictures its uses include the representation of fields, sand and thatched roofs. It is one of the easier veneers to cut.

AMERICAN GUM

Found only in the United States of America, this veneer is a pinkish-red colour with grey-brown streaks which very often form a swirly figuration. It also has a wide pale sapwood. It has a feel much like magnolia with, if anything, a finer, more even texture, which cuts easily. It also has a beautiful lustre.

With a little imagination this veneer can form a complete picture, the right figuring producing foregound, horizon and sky (see second colour section). It is also a favourite veneer for costumery.

ASH (EUROPEAN)

This wood grows in Europe and Canada. It is off-white to cream in colour with a somewhat lustrous straight grain. If quarter cut it sometimes has a heavy fiddleback-type mottle or a wide wavy figure if crown cut. It is very brittle when cut across the grain markings, although the wide plain veneer between the grain marks can be a delight to work with.

European ash makes for very fine sky effects as well as distant mountains and wild life subjects, and the closer figured veneer is also ideal for water effects. It also sand shades beautifully and hence is ideal to use on floral subjects.

Japanese ash (tamo) is darker, varying from brownish-tan to grey. The grain can be highly varied with swirls, mottle and a peanut shell figure. Both varieties can be tough on knife points.

OLIVE ASH

A European wood, olive ash is similar to both European and American white ash, but with light brown streaks which make it much more attractive. The bottom or butt end of the log is most attractive with its wild, wavy figuring.

It does not need very much imagination to see waves in water in this wood, and this is what it is best used for. The streaky parts can also make a stunning sky effect and it can give an effective interpretation of shadow effects on paths and roads. The close striped pieces are good for depicting fencing and wooden planks.

The veneer can be quite coarse and is sometimes brittle to cut; watch for 'shelly' pieces (thick and thin patches which you can see if you hold it up to the light). It sand shades well.

ASPEN

Aspen grows in the USA and Canada. This veneer is usually produced from very large logs and comes in quite big sheets, sometimes with 75–100 mm (3–4 in.) of sapwood which is almost white in colour while the heartwood is yellowish-orange with golden-cream streaks, often with a fiddleback mottle in the grain.

Many pictures are started using aspen as a waster-background or sky-effect veneer, but using it as sky can be a mistake as a fiddleback mottle can look aerodynamically wrong with the mottle running vertically through the grain.

Aspen is very easy to cut (always a bonus) and sand shades well.

AVODIRE

A West African wood, avodire is yellow-cream to pale gold in colour with a wavy secondary grain running at a slight angle to the main grain with which it interlocks. As a result of this grain structure, avodire has a beautiful lustre and its fine grain is also easy to cut. It comes in very wide pieces, often over 300 mm (12 in.), and because of this it makes a superb sky waster.

Because it sand shades well it is ideal for flowers, leaves and costumes, but it is also used for fields, one face of Louis cubes and cross-grained borders.

MASUR BIRCH

Found all over northern Europe, this wood is creamy-white in colour with strange dark brown stringy flecks which give an effect similar to birds-eye maple. The veneer is soft and pliable and easy to cut with no definite grain direction to pull the knife point away from its intended course. With its unusual grain it could easily be mistaken for a burr. It sand shades easily.

Masur birch is best used to represent roadside walls, pebble roads and paths and sea-shores.

CASTELLA

A wood from South America and the West Indies, this is a fine close-grained veneer with a smooth satin surface. The grain is the main feature of this wood which on a pale to golden brown background gives greyish-olive colour markings which are often wild and wavy and which make the veneer ideal for water and sea subjects. It is possible to obtain sheets of this veneer which require the minimum of subject matter to produce a picture, and many marquetarians would claim that this is the true art of marquetry, using the veneer to its greatest effect rather than cutting in minute detail. It is also ideal for costumes and drapery, cornfields, thatched roofs and leaves on floral subjects.

Castella is generally an easy veneer to cut but can sometimes flake and splinter when cut with the grain. The veneer without the wild, wavy markings is sold under the name of boxwood.

'Receding Tide', the picture on page 11, is a good example of the use of castella.

CEDAR OF LEBANON or LEBANON CEDAR

Grown in the Middle East, this timber is biscuit to yellowish-gold in colour with tints of pink. It is a highly resinous wood and you can almost feel the dampness. The resin is strongly scented and this fact alone makes it a must for all veneer collections. The growth rings are well defined, usually with narrow crown figuring flanked by stripy grain.

Its best uses are for costumes, drapery, barn walls and distant fields as well as the crown-cut veneer making very effective skies.

The veneer sand shades well but, in common with many other veneers which have low density, it may drag and crumble on the cut edges.

EUROPEAN CHERRY

This is found throughout Europe and North Africa. It is pale pink to biscuit in colour, which makes it very useful for portraiture, and is basically straight-grained with a very narrow figuring down the centre of the log, the figuring moving quickly from one side of the leaf to the other so that great care and thought are needed when this area is used. It is also susceptible to black marks which suddenly appear and then disappear.

European cherry is close grained and easy to cut. It is worth looking out for leaves from the beginning of the log which can often be very sappy and are more of a creamy-pastel yellow in colour, sometimes with freak markings.

HORSE CHESTNUT

This comes from the United Kingdom, Europe and some parts of Asia. It is almost white in colour and very, very soft with almost no grain marks to speak of and as a result it is one of the easiest veneers to cut accurately. It is an ideal waster when a very light, featureless background is required as well as blank skies and snow scenes.

The veneer sand shades very well but this must be done with care as it scorches very quickly. Care must also be taken when preparing the surface for polishing as it will sand through very easily. Also, without protection, its whiteness is lost over a period of time, strong daylight turning the veneer a creamy-yellow colour.

Horse chestnut is a good veneer to treat to produce harewood.

SWEET CHESTNUT

This wood is also found in the United Kingdom and Europe. It looks very much like oak but without the silver streaks in the grain. Light tan in colour, it is

softer than oak but the grain is very coarse to cut and can be hard on knife points.

This is not a widely used veneer but it can be used effectively for distant fields and various other parts of landscapes, and for wooden subjects (often the most difficult things to represent with a veneer!).

EBONY (MACASSAR)

This is grown in the island of Celebes, one of the Indonesian islands, whose southern capital is Macassar. Ebony is often assumed to be totally black but this is not so: some pieces have only streaks of black on a pale brown, beige or dark grey background. It is a very difficult veneer to cut, being very hard and brittle, and you can be forgiven for thinking that a mallet and chisel are the best tools to use.

Ebony makes good borders if cut into strips and is ideal for stringers around the edge of pictures if you can get it cut into thin strips about 1–2 mm ($^1/_{32}$–$^1/_8$ ins.) wide. It is also a good veneer for making the dark squares on chess-boards. It can be seen forming one of the alternative skies in our step-by-step picture in the second colour section, but in general our advice would be to leave it to those who use the fretsaw technique.

ELM

Found in the United Kingdom and Europe, elm veneer is pale brown, sometimes with a reddish-brown tinge, and often has a greenish cast in the straight grain. It has an open coarse grain which can be a nightmare to cut as it is very hard on knife points and tends to drag the knife along with it. This makes it difficult to cut accurately, especially straight along the grain, even if you use a rule or metal straight edge.

The 'quarter' cut veneer produces a straight grain, which makes a very good ploughed field effect. It can also be used to produce a thatched roof effect as well as doors and planked fences, but is not used very much and the beginner would be advised to avoid it.

EUCALYPTUS

An Australian wood. This genus produces a great variety of woods with a wide range of textures and colours. The sample pictured in the first colour section is the most commonly available and is cream to buff in colour with a heavy box-type mottle which can make the veneer feel like flattened corrugated cardboard, and means it is difficult to cut.

Eucalyptus is used mainly for landscape fields and stone walls.

This handsome veneer also comes in a deep pink to red which is called rose eucalyptus but has all the characteristics typical of eucalyptus.

HAREWOOD

This is a false veneer as it is a veneer which has been chemically treated. Sycamore, maple, beech, yew, masur birch, ash and planetree are all woods with a high tannin content which will react when it comes into contact with ferrous sulphate and turns the veneer any shade between silver grey and dark slate grey. Soaking your veneer in a tea solution before soaking it in the ferrous sulphate can extend the range of greys that you can create. But beware using the ferrous sulphate technique with oak, which is tempting due to the dark marine blue which it appears to produce, as you will find that this will scrape or sand off easily as it is not absorbed right into the wood. Before using any harewood, in fact, it is advisable to check the penetration of the reaction; seeing a dark grey turn pale at the sanding-down stage of a piece of work can be a heart-breaking experience.

Harewood and black-dyed veneer are the only false colours we would propose that you use. Dyed veneer (reds, blues, greens, etc.) can look very out of place among the natural colours and they tend to be very flat with little grain or tone graduations.

Harewood has a wide range of uses and its popularity is enhanced by the fact that it is usually produced from veneers which are easy to cut; this is because these are the woods which absorb the chemical well. Sky and water are obvious uses, but it also looks good as distant hills, metallic objects, windows, and blossom (in bird's eye maple harewood).

Sand shading is not successful with harewood as the veneer turns brown rather than a darker grey. Make sure all veneers are fully dried before attempting to sand shade.

HOLLY

Found all over Europe and the USA, holly is a very white veneer, in fact probably the whitest available, with almost no visible grain pattern. It has a very fine, even texture which can be a bit tough to cut but will hold together well if cut into intricate shapes.

Most logs of holly will be small and most leaves of veneer no wider than 100–150 mm (4 –6 in.).

This is an ideal wood for snow scenes and floral subjects as well as highlights on all manner of subjects including eyes. It also sand shades well and is often found in bought inlay motifs (Sheraton ovals, shells and fans). Look out for veneers from a naturally stained log as these offer very interesting grey-black marble-type markings which are excellent for draped cloth, as well as distant hills, birds' feathers, etc.

HORNBEAM

Found all over Europe and Asia, hornbeam is a dull white with the occasional greyish tinge and sometimes also has bluish stains. It is very much like holly in nature, having no real grain pattern and being very hard and only available in narrow pieces. With some patience it cuts nicely as there are no problems with crumbling or splintering.

Hornbeam works well with holly as the shadow effect against the whiteness of the holly. It also sand shades well, which makes it ideal for floral subjects.

INDIAN SILVER GREY

A wood from the Andaman Islands in the Indian Ocean. The colour is olive grey with dark grey, sometimes almost black, markings. These markings are often straight but some pieces have good figuring which resembles some walnuts in appearance. However the grain is much coarser and more brittle to cut than walnut and can crumble when cut into intricate shapes.

Its colour and figuring mean that it is popular for depicting leaves, fields, thatched roofs and water effects.

KHAYA

A North African wood, this veneer is pale pink to red-brown in colour and has a medium texture with an interlocked grain typically associated with mahogany; it can be straight grained (quarter cut) or figured and is obtainable in very wide sheets.

Most sheets of this veneer are unattractive to the marquetarian and as a result is mainly used as a 'balancer' (on the back of pictures, etc.). Usually known in the veneer trade as 'bastard mahogany.'

KOTO

From West Africa, Koto is creamy-yellowish in colour with a rather dull appearance. It resembles a 'white mahogany' in nature in having an interlocking grain structure. It is very porous and soft and as a result can drag and crumble when cut, much as does obeche which has a similar structure.

Its uses are limited in pictures, except for landscaped fields and as shadows when used with sycamore or maple.

MAGNOLIA

This is sometimes known as 'cucumber wood' and comes mainly from the USA. Magnolia is the only available true green (more of a pastel green) since the green Cyprus burr is now very rare. It has a very 'easy' figure with almost white sapwood, but it is well worth looking out for the odd log that has been stained by minerals in the soil as these can produce markings containing blue to almost black as well as purple/lilac and dark green streaks. A burr is sometimes available which is a darker shade of green than the normal veneer. Magnolia is very easy to cut.

Its main use is for leaves on floral subjects, grass hills on landscapes, and still life studies such as apples and grapes. It is also used wherever a hint of green is required. Magnolia sand shades well, and can be made a slightly darker shade of green if laid on top of the hot sand and removed just before it scorches.

Problems can arise if the veneer is left on a bench where it is exposed to sunlight as this will in time turn the veneer an olive brown colour.

MAHOGANY

A name often misapplied to veneers not of the mahogany family.

African mahogany
From the Gold Coast, this is pink to reddish-brown in colour with a lavish figure, and is also available with a mottle, fiddleback and with fine curls.

Cuban mahogany
From Cuba and the West Indies, this veneer is light brown or tan when cut, darkening to a deep rich red-brown, and is highly figured.

Brazilian mahogany
This veneer is from tropical America and is a rich orange-brown.

Honduras mahogany
This mahogany is light brown in colour like Khaya.

Philippine mahogany
A pink-brown veneer which is the poor relation of the mahogany family!

All the mahoganies are worth collecting if the chance arises, purely for the slight differences in the colour and grain markings.

MAKORE

A wood from Nigeria, this is often known as cherry makore. It is pinkish-brown to blood red in colour, and somewhat similar to mahogany, with a broad straight interlocked grain but with the smaller pores found in cherry. A fine-textured wood which is hard and often gummy but very lustrous.

Floral subjects, roofs and borders are among its uses, but beware, when sanded the dust can be an irritant to the nose and throat.

MAPLE

This wood is found all over the USA, Canada and Europe. It is cream-white to light tan in colour with red-brown figuring, often wild with no obvious direction. The figuring can move a considerable distance through the thickness of a veneer making it difficult to select small areas of required marking with the normal method, on the reverse side.

Maple makes beautiful skies, the figuring forming ready-made clouds. Pieces chosen well can make fine floral subjects which are enhanced by its good sand-shading properties.

MAPLE – BIRD'S EYE

From Canada and the USA. Light cream to pinkish cream in colour, it is highly figured with a wavy grain and scattered over the entire tree are eye-like knots making it almost like a burr. Normally, because of the smallness of the tree, it is half-round cut or rotary cut (a lathe-like action) which peels the veneer off in one long leaf which is later separated into individual leaves.

It makes an ideal veneer for snow scenes, flowers and floral designs, and drapery.

OAK – EUROPEAN

This species of oak is found not only in Europe but also in Asia and North Africa. It is cream to light tan in colour with white-greyish tinges in the heartwood. We have found very little use for this veneer in marquetry and conclude that it is best left to cabinet-maker's, with whom it enjoys a wide popularity, and to architectural veneering.

This is a very brittle and sometimes difficult veneer to cut because of the deep grain markings.

OAK – BROWN

A much more interesting veneer than European oak, being deep gold to dark brown in colour with interesting markings in dark brown to black.

A much easier veneer to cut than European (white) oak and somewhat more useful because of its mottled dark markings. It is ideal for bird's plumage and animal subjects in general.

OAK – BOG

This veneer is totally black as a result of being buried in peat bogs or in river silt for a long time; in some cases samples are 1000 – 2000 years old.

It looks forbidding but is usually the easiest of the oaks to cut, perhaps because of its past moisture content. Due to its very open structure it is not an easy veneer to finish to a smooth unpitted surface and a dyed veneer or harewood is usually preferred.

OPEPE

A West African wood, this veneer is a very distinctive bright orange to yellow colour. It has an interlocked grain and a mottle which runs across the grain in an irregular pattern. Having a very coarse grain makes it very difficult to cut without it splintering and crumbling, and it is wise to use sticky tape on at least one surface before attempting to cut it.

The grain resembles fur and hence it is good for animal subjects, especially tigers.

ANDAMAN PADUAK

Andaman paduak comes solely from the Andaman Islands. It is an attractive wood, bright red to crimson in colour, but one which can create a lot of problems. In veneer form it is very brittle, tending to crumble when cut with the knife, and requires sticky tape to hold it together; if this is still not successful rubbing PVA adhesive into the surface will give further support to the brittle grain structure. The hardness of the wood also means it is very hard on knife tips.

But the problems do not end here! During the finishing processes the paduak will bleed into the surrounding wood causing a pinkish mist or a pink halo, especially in light-coloured soft-grained veneers. To prevent this the veneer must be sealed with the finishing product (cellulose-based sanding sealer for example) by painting the individual Paduak veneers with the sealer and allowing it to dry thoroughly before painting adjacent veneers.

Paduak is commonly used for house roofs, boat sails, flower petals and costumes.

PEAR

From both Europe and Asia, this light to mid-pink veneer has a very fine texture which makes it very easy to cut intricate shapes (it's almost like cutting cardboard).

Because of its colour it is ideal for portraiture and costume subjects. It also sand shades very well and this makes it excellent for flower petals. Pear is also a good alternative colour for Louis cubes because it has a natural lustre.

It is also available with a very heavy fiddleback-type mottle on narrow leaves.

PLANETREE

A widely distributed tree found throughout Europe, Asia and Australia. This veneer is light pink to red in colour and has a straight-grained even texture, but can be flaky when cut due to a fleck structure in the grain. It is also known as lacewood because when quarter cut it can reveal rays in the timber which produce a very distinctive fleck figure, often quite large. Planetree veneer can sometimes resemble beech.

Because of its fleck pattern it is mainly used for stone walls, paths and roads and can also be used in portraiture.

PURPLE HEART

A Central and South American wood. Sometimes this veneer is called violetwood: it is a dull brown in colour when first cut but then turns a deep true purple. This makes it one of the most distinctive and vividly coloured of all woods but be warned, if given prolonged exposure to bright daylight it returns to a dull brown. it is also one of the woods with a reflective ripple which runs across the grain in a rather random pattern.

The veneer is often sliced very thick, which makes

it very difficult to cut with the knife. It makes good stringers and bandings as well as being very good for flower subjects and drapery.

RIO ROSEWOOD

Rio Rosewood comes from Brazil in various shades of dark brown, chocolate and sometimes even violet, with many black streaks. Often it has a wide, pale sapwood area which is usually pale straw in colour. It has rather large open pores, like wenge, which make it hard to cut and finish. It is still a worthwhile veneer to have available though, and especially useful is the part where the sapwood merges with the heartwood.

SAPELE

From West Africa, in particular Nigeria, this veneer is pink-brown to dark red-brown in colour. It has what is called a 'pencil' stripe because it is quarter cut and these stripes can vary from very narrow to very wide, and the interlocking grain produces a highly lustrous finish when polished. As the finished veneer is viewed from various angles the light-dark stripes change in reflective quality and hence appear to change in colour.

It is used mainly in the cabinet-making industry and hence is widely available. Because of its straight narrow stripes it makes ideal borders, both long and cross grain, for pictures and cabinet doors. It makes a very good veneer for Louis cubes and lattice work designs.

Sapele can be seen on the television cabinet doors (see second colour section).

SAPELE – CROWN CUT

This wood comes from West Africa and is the same timber as sapele but cut right through the log to produce a striking heavy-figured cathedral-type grain of dark red-brown colour, often with a mottle or fiddleback markings. From the 'crotch' of the tree we get curls, a highly decorative veneer used in cabinet-making.

It is used for much the same purposes as utile or sapele, and is an easy veneer to cut. It is better not to use it as a border unless you have four matching pieces, otherwise it can make your picture look lopsided.

SATINWOOD

This veneer, from Sri Lanka, is pale to golden yellow in colour with a straight stripe and running across the grain is what is usually called a bees' wing mottle. It is hard to cut and is hard on knife points. The veneer often has gum marks and this wood can be an irritant to the skin.

It sand shades very well which makes it ideal for floral subjects and drapery. Borders and fancy bandings are other popular uses.

SYCAMORE

This is a wood found growing in Europe and Asia. It is white to creamy-white in colour and when quarter cut very often has a heavy fiddleback mottle whereas flat cut sycamore has a wide soft cathedral-type figuring which occasionally also possesses the fiddleback. It has a very close grain which makes it a delight to cut and it will also stand up to cutting into very intricate shapes without breaking. It is wise to collect as many pieces of sycamore as possible because the shades of colour differ with every sample and it has such a wide range of uses.

Being one of the whitest veneers available in large flat sheets makes it ideal for cutting stringers, light squares on chess-boards, sky effects, and for wasters because of its good cutting properties. Because of its natural lustre it is also yet another alternative for Louis cubes.

A by-product of sycamore is weathered sycamore which is produced by steaming; this changes the colour to a light to medium brown.

AFRICAN WALNUT

A West African wood, also known as Nigerian walnut, this is closely related to mahogany. It has a warm golden-brown colour with a straight interlocked grain, very much like pencil-striped sapele mahogany. It is easy to cut. African Walnut is sometimes crown cut which produces a not very attractive, rather dead-looking figure similar to crown-cut mahogany.

It is best suited for cross-banding borders, also fields in landscapes, thatched roofs, etc., and is another good veneer for Louis cubes.

AMERICAN WALNUT

This comes from the United States and Canada. The grain is a little coarser than that of European walnut and its colour is generally much darker, varying from

European Ash (all veneers to this scale)

Olive Ash

Aspen

Avodire

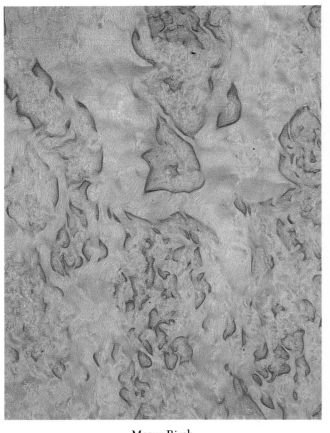

Masur Birch

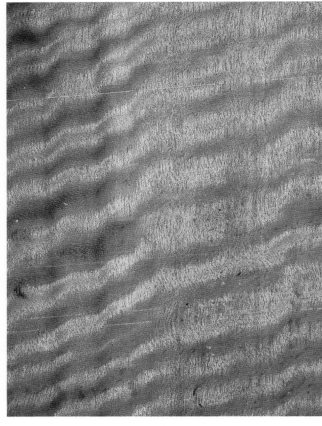

Eucalyptus

Harewood

Indian Silver Grey

Magnolia

Makore

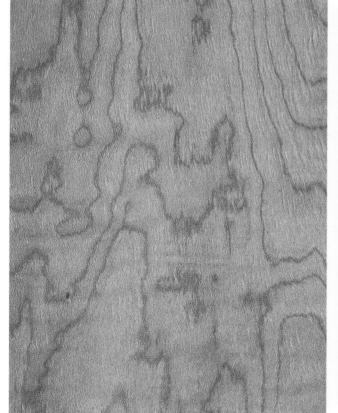

Maple

Brown Oak

Andaman Paduak

Pear

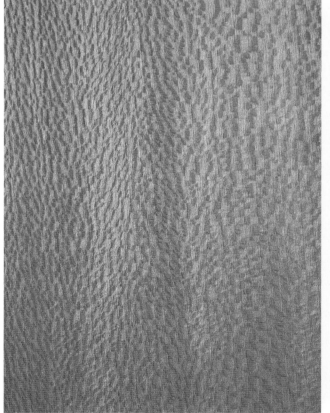

Planetree

Purple Heart

Rio Rosewood

Sapele – Crown Cut

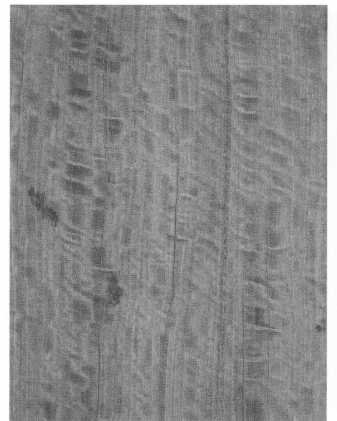

Satinwood

African Walnut

American Walnut

European Walnut

Wenge

Willow

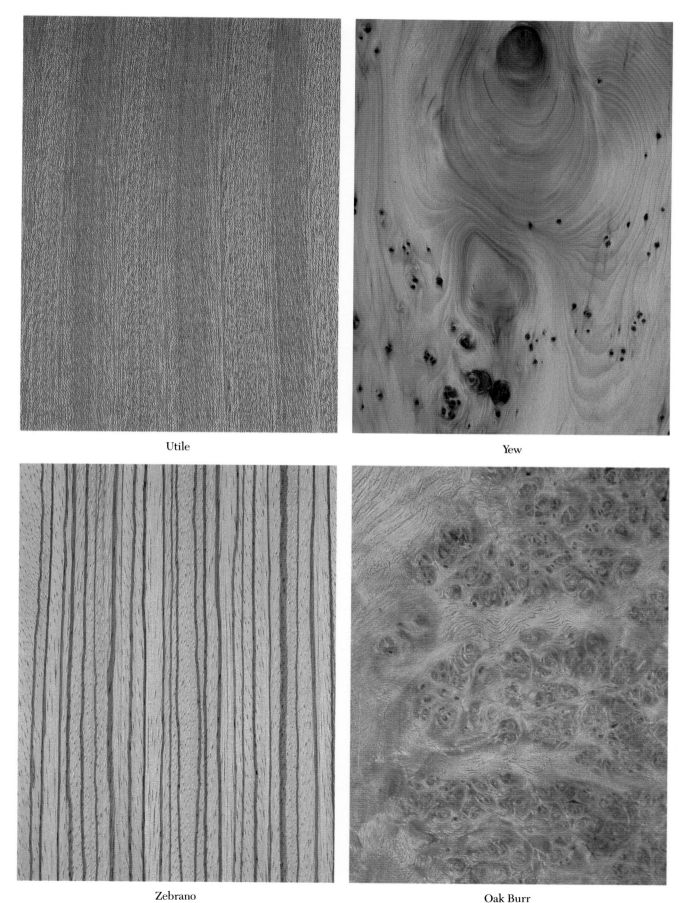

Utile

Yew

Zebrano

Oak Burr

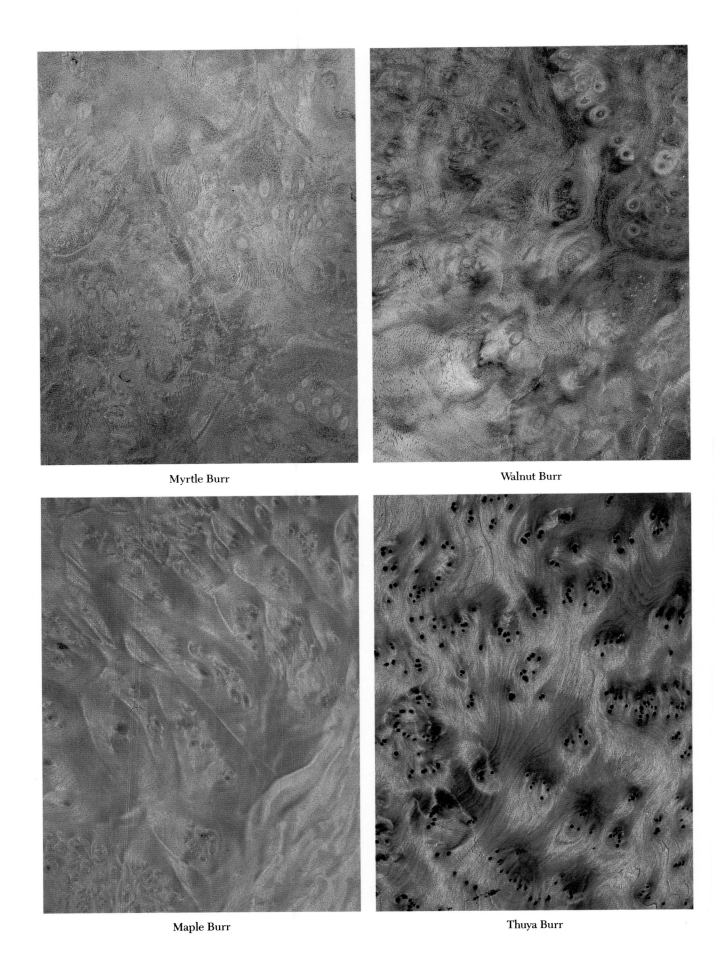

Myrtle Burr

Walnut Burr

Maple Burr

Thuya Burr

dark brown to purple to almost black. It is also not quite as highly figured as its European relation apart from the butt ends, and although it is also not quite as easy to cut it is another must for your veneer collection.

EUROPEAN WALNUT

This timber is found in England, France and Italy and parts of Asia. No veneer collection should be without as many pieces as can be afforded. Its merit is in its diversity of colour and figuring, and because of its lack of definite grain direction and its softness it cuts beautifully. The sapwood is ideal as a waster due to its cutting qualities, and with the heartwood varying from light grey to light dark brown, which may include streaks of almost black, the subject matter to which this veneer can be applied is almost limitless.

WENGE

Grown in the Cameroon and Zaire, Wenge is a hard dark brown, almost black wood which has an open and coarse grain which makes it difficult to cut and polish. Dust from sanding can enter into the open pores and prove very difficult to get rid of.

Best uses are for stringers and bandings which should be cut with a long-bladed knife to try to prevent it from splintering and crumbling. Not a veneer for the beginner!

WILLOW

Willow is grown in Europe, America, Africa and Asia. Often known as moiree, it is white-cream to biscuit in colour, usually with a straight grain, but looks highly figured because of a mottled curly water-ripple effect which runs parallel at 90° to the grain direction.

This veneer is very easy to cut, is soft and smooth to the touch and sand shades beautifully which makes it very effective when used on floral subjects, for example petals on roses, and for costumes. The whitest pieces can be used for snow scenes and water effects.

UTILE

Utile is found in East and West Africa. This veneer is very much like sapele in appearance but is coarser with an interlocked grain and much wider stripes which mean that it is not so decorative. It is very easy to cut and is dark red to brown in colour.

It is another veneer which can be used for Louis cubes as well as the usual range of subjects like roofs. Utile can also be used for borders and is sometimes used as a balancer for pictures.

YEW

A widely spread tree found in the United Kingdom, Europe, Asia, Africa and India. This is another wood veneer with many colours, the sapwood ranging from almost white to bright yellow and the heartwood tan through to orange, frequently streaked with purple, mauve and red.

It can also have clusters of tiny black knots and a swirling grain and can be frustrating due to its tendency to have areas of ingrowing bark which result in large holes in the sheets of veneer. Yew can be crumbly to cut, it tends to flake off on the cut edge, but if this problem can be overcome it is a most useful part of a veneer collection.

ZEBRANO

From the Gabon region of Africa, zebrano is a highly decorative and exceptionally distinctive wood. It is straw coloured with pronounced fine dark brown, almost black, close stripes and a very lustrous appearance. A very hard wood, it is difficult to cut, especially across the grain.

It makes ideal veneer for fences, sheds, barns and any wooden subjects, and gives a very fine ploughed field effect.

CURLS, CLUSTERS, BURRS AND BUTTS

These are the names of certain cuts of veneers taken from specific parts of the tree.

CURLS

These are cut from the part of the tree that divides into the first two main branches, called the crotch. This produces a cathedral-type figure with a pronounced scar running through the middle, sometimes known as a rat's tail or flame effect. These veneers are much sought after in the cabinet-making trade for antique reproduction furniture.

Curls are available in several veneers including mahogany (African), mahogany (khaya) – which is more of a swirl, avodire – which is used as a substitute for mahogany and is usually stained, and American walnut. Curls are rarely more than about 1.3 m (4 ft) in length.

CLUSTERS

This is the name given to veneer that has small burr-like growths up and down the length of the trunk which are not big enough to be cut as burrs. The best known are oak and poplar or mappa clusters.

Oak cluster

A figured oak with small areas of knots. The veneer itself can be difficult to use as it tends to buckle badly around the knotty areas and it can also be shelly and splintery as well as thin in some areas.

Poplar or mappa cluster

Another popular variety, white to cream in colour with wild swirly grain and hundreds of dark brown to black knots in large patches. Apart from some knots which tend to drop out immediately after being sliced into veneer it is usually quite sound and easy to cut.

BURRS

These are growths or carbuncles that grow on the trunk of the tree, usually around the crotch area, and are covered with short fine twigs. In some species these can grow quite large (elm, oak, walnut) while others may be very small (maple, amboyna, yew). The range is limited to about 15–25 species that are cut for industrial use.

Burrs are much sought after and because of this you can sometimes expect to pay a lot for the smallest piece. Some species, for example green Cyprus burr, are becoming quite difficult to get hold of.

When cut, these veneers are a mass of tiny knots and swirly grain, often needing a lot of attention to patch and make sound areas that are missing because of ingrowing bark or other defects.

The main use for burrs in marquetry is in trees and foliage, stone walls, animal subjects and hair in portraiture. Trees in a burr can be particularly effective if sufficient cutting is carried out, even though they are not green.

Green burrs

The only true green veneer is Cyprus burr, but another greenish burr worth keeping an eye out for is magnolia burr which is a good substitute.

Oak burr

Sometimes the knots in this burr will appear in small clusters over a large area. It can be one of the most brittle and hard of veneers.

Myrtle burr

By comparison with oak burr this is soft and easily worked and is olive gold in colour.

Walnut burr

This is perhaps the easiest to obtain and one of the most popular, partly because of its good cutting properties. It can be very dark brown/grey with swirly black marks among the knots.

Maple burr

This veneer is quite unlike the white maple being pinkish-red in colour and is very easy to cut.

Thuya burr

From North Africa, specifically Algeria, this veneer has a reddish-brown swirly figure with many tiny black pips (knots) much like yew burr. It is one of the few burrs grown under the ground, as part of the root, the tree being cut back to force greater growth below ground level.

The burr is cut very thick, probably because of its crumbly nature. It is a very decorative wood with an aromatic scent which makes it much prized for the lining of cigar boxes. This veneer is very hard to cut into intricate shapes with a knife and is best left to this use.

BUTTS

The butts are cut from the base of the tree just above the roots and hence are a relatively small proportion of the useful timber. As well as having rarity value the butt is sought after for its grain which is much more wild and interesting than that of the rest of the trunk. The butt is beautifully marked with a combination of mottled, swirly and knotty grain markings ranging from black to slate grey, brown to beige, with no discernible grain direction. Butts are easily worked and when four quartered will produce a breathtaking kaleidoscope of patterns. Among the most popular are American walnut, European walnut, olive ash, elm and brown oak.

4

Basic Methods

There are various cutting methods in common use in marquetry but we have concentrated on the window method as the most satisfactory for the average marquetarian. Other methods have certain disadvantages.

STICK-AS-YOU-GO

The stick-as-you-go method, as detailed in marquetry kits, relies on a very accurate transfer of lines from a drawing to the individual pieces of veneer using carbon paper. Tracing the same line twice to an accuracy of about 0.2 mm (0.01 in.) is an almost impossible task, and the subsequent cutting can only increase the errors. This method results in poor joints and a limited design range. Also, the marks of the carbon paper are on the face of the picture and may remain to stain the surface permanently.

THE FRETSAW

Another method employs a fretsaw to cut the veneer. In the multiple-layer process the veneer is cut to a pattern through several leaves and then fitted together like jigsaw pieces. Very little can be done about taking care in the selection of veneers for grain direction, coloration or figuring. Also, the saw cuts have width and are often used to produce lines through the cut forms. At mounting the adhesive fills the cuts and the gaps between the pieces of veneer and the result is a series of dark lines between mating pieces. This can look attractive but is a little crude.

Much better results can be obtained by a similar method which cuts only two mating pieces at any one time. A smaller gap is achieved by making the cut at about 7° to the normal cutting plane. This is obtained by maintaining the saw blade in the vertical axis and supporting the veneer at an angle of about 7° to the horizontal: the actual angle can be determined by simple trigonometry as shown in Fig. 15. The result is a slightly angled joint which, when the parts are fitted together, gives a flush joint with a perfect close fit. A very fine blade is required for this work (004 – 006) and particular care is required at sharp corners to ensure a perfect fit. Fig. 16 shows the principle of the technique.

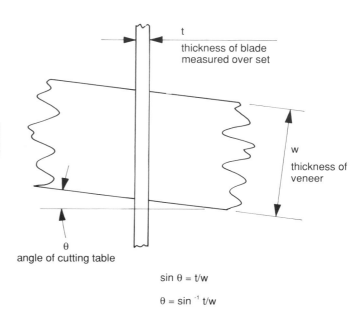

$$\sin \theta = t/w$$

$$\theta = \sin^{-1} t/w$$

Fig. 15 Calculating the cutting table angle for the mechanical saw or donkey

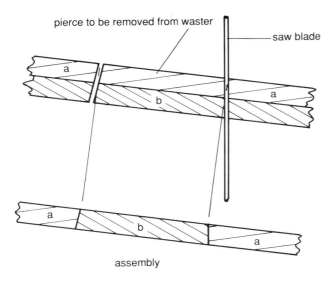

pierce to be removed from waster

saw blade

a

b

a

a

b

a

assembly

Fig. 16 *Sawing and assembly using the donkey or home made equipment*

THE DONKEY

Professional marquetarians use a very similar method but the fretsaw is replaced by the 'Donkey'. The main advantages of this machine are as follows:

- It leaves both hands free to control the sheets of veneer, often quite large.
- It has a deep throat to cope with large sheets of veneer.
- The blade moves in a vertical plane and as a result cutting should be more accurate and the blades will have a longer life.

Its disadvantages are that it is a large machine which takes up a lot of space. It is also very expensive.

It is possible to adapt a deep-throated fretsaw to a treadle-driven system or even a power drive through a geared-down electric motor. The frame is pivoted at its top end and the blade guided by a hardened steel plate to prevent lateral movement and give a vertical cut at the cutting plane.

THE VIBRO SAW

The Vibro saw works on the principle of a high-frequency vibration of the saw blade, which is the same as used in a fretsaw, with a very small vertical movement. It will cut through any solid sheet material, within reason, if the correct blade is fitted. It cannot however cope with veneer with any

flexibility, which simply shatters as it flexes against the cutting edge of the blade.

THE WINDOW METHOD

This method has a number of advantages. It is not necessary to follow a design with such extreme accuracy, which gives you the freedom to alter shapes to suit the grain pattern of the selected veneer or to follow a whim of artistic creativity, or even to cover up a cutting error. Cutting small shapes freehand without having to transfer all the fine detail to the waster which exists on the original design can save time and be far less restrictive.

The matching piece to the jigsaw is shaped to fit the hole in the waster, guided by the window, and hence great accuracy can be achieved.

The most important advantage is the ability to place the veneer behind the window and hence view it as it will be seen before cutting it. As a result the colour, grain, texture, shading, etc. can be compared to that of adjacent veneers and to the original design, which makes selection much easier and more satisfactory. It also means that should you change your mind about any selected, cut and glued veneer at any time before mounting, the piece can be cut out and replaced with what you consider to be a more appropriate choice.

METHOD

We will start from the point where a design has been transferred on to the *back* of our starting sheet of veneer, which we call the waster. (The process in getting this far is described in the step-by-step guide in Chapter 8). You can use card as a waster at this stage on the grounds that it is more homogeneous to work on and hence it will be easier to make a true cut. However the abrasive nature of card will soon take the edge off a keen-bladed knife and in fact the card can be much more difficult to cut than a suitably selected waster veneer. Sapwood from walnut (or sap walnut) is ideal although if the waster is to be used to give a sky effect it will be necessary to use a light veneer such as aspen, sycamore or maple, all of which cut well.

Cutting the window

Start by cutting the furthermost objects. Selecting the shape to be cut out, draw the knife round the outline keeping the blade square to the veneer and holding it almost like a pencil with a relatively small amount of the knife protruding from the fingers – the further up the handle you hold the knife the less control you are going to have. Don't try to cut through the veneer in one pass of the knife. Accuracy is more important than speed and a light cut makes it possible to control the tip of the blade to follow closely the marked line. When doing this never twist the blade while it is stationary in the veneer as it will result in the tip of the blade snapping off. Also rotate the veneer as often as is required for a comfortable cutting direction rather than twist yourself about too much so that you lose control. Standing can be an advantage when cutting difficult shapes as it gives more manoeuvrability. After the initial light cut you can increase the pressure and repeat the cut until the piece falls free.

Points to remember

- Try to avoid angling the knife sideways; the blade should remain square to the veneer.
- Try to keep the knife at about 60° to the veneer in the direction of cut (see Fig. 19) Smaller angles are only suitable for straight lines and larger angles make the knife difficult to hold.
- Always cut away from the internal corners to prevent the blade accidently cutting into the waster, or more importantly the inserted veneers, as the work progresses.

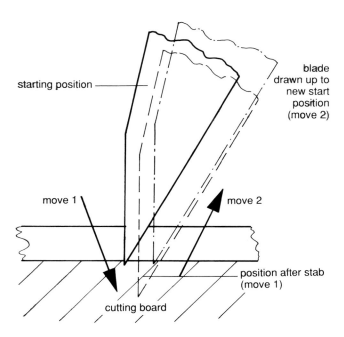

Fig. 17   Sequence of cuts for stab method

[Diagram labels: starting position; blade drawn up to new start position (move 2); move 1; move 2; position after stab (move 1); cutting board]

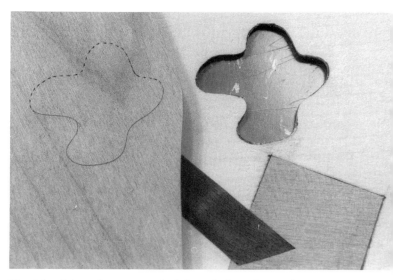

Fig. 18   Selected veneer marked through from the window in the waster by the stab method

- Always remove the piece of veneer with a clean cut, never forcing it out as you will leave yourself with a ragged torn edge. By inspecting the face side of the veneer it is possible to detect where the cut is incomplete.

Should the cut be too convoluted or the veneer too hard to be cut by drawing the blade along the line, it may be necessary to use the 'stab' method. This involves pushing the point of the blade into the veneer, extracting it and drawing it forward a little ready to push in again. If the tip of the blade remains in the cut the effect is to produce a continuous cut rather than a series of perforations, and although it take a little extra time the cut will be complete after one final pass of the knife. Fig. 17 attempts to illustrate the sequence of pushing down into the veneer and drawing up along the cut, and Fig. 18 shows the effect of the stab method with a rather exaggerated distance between the stabs. This process has several advantages:

- Complex shapes can be cut with little cutting skill.
- The knife is unlikely to slip off the line.
- The danger of the blade tip breaking is reduced as there is no need to twist the blade while you are actually cutting.

Any ragged edges must be cleaned up before you continue with the next part of the process.

Fitting in the veneer

What we have now formed is a window into which a piece of veneer must be fitted accurately. After making the initial selection of veneer place the sheet behind the window, still working with the face side down. The selection of grain direction, figuring, spacing, and tone range can now be made by sliding and rotating the selected veneer about under the window. Should no suitable view present itself then further veneer selections can be made and manipulated behind the window until the desired effect is observed.

Note

Once you have begun to glue the pieces of cut veneer into the windows the veneers on the working face (which will become the back face) will darken. Excessive use of carbon paper and glue application, as well as general grime, may darken the veneer so much that it is almost impossible to follow the transferred design. So work as cleanly as possible and clear away any excess glue quickly with the heel of the blade. The inevitable darkening of the veneers on the working side can also lead to the problem that you select veneers a few shades darker than is required for the contrast necessary and following

this all subsequent veneers become darker in an effort to maintain contrast.

To avoid ending up with an excess of dark woods (which are moreover difficult to cut) keep checking the colour and tone against the face side of the marquetry which should remain clean throughout.

Having chosen a veneer and placed it under the window hold it in place with draughting or masking tape in three places, back or front.

We find beginners tend to cut out a small square of their selected veneer and tape this in place. The result is that they tend to use the veneer in a strict order, without looking for the most suitable grain. Wastage is also quite high with this method as the material left is only fit to be thrown away. It is much better to leave the veneer in one piece, cutting out pieces as required. A well-used veneer will look like a piece of lace before it is discarded.

To cut the veneer through the window

We now come to the element requiring the greatest skill, cutting the veneer through the window. It is

Fig. 19 Making the first cut

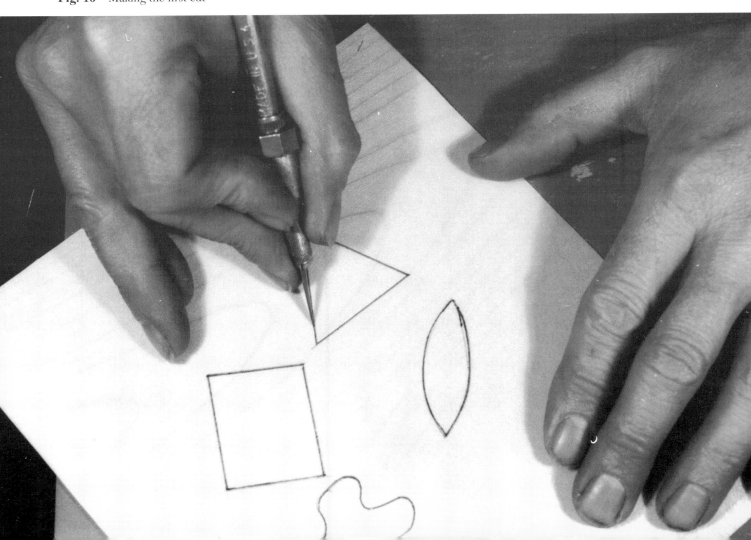

Fig. 20   Cutting through the window

difficult to describe, relatively easy to demonstrate, but only practice will make perfect, preferably with personal tuition from a skilled marquetarian. Many people are put off marquetry when they attempt their first picture, having been presented with a marquetry kit. The amount of veneer supplied in a kit gives no latitude for practice before you attempt your first cuts into a picture. Anyone in this situation would be well advised to purchase a few extra sheets of veneer to use as practice pieces. The series of illustrations Figs. 19 to 24 shows a typical practice exercise.

The piece of practice veneer is marked with four shapes. These can be drawn straight on to the veneer with a pencil, and if this were a design this would be the **back** face which would eventually be glued to the mounting board. Keep the shapes simple to start with and use a veneer which cuts well (e.g. aspen, magnolia, maple, sycamore, sap walnut).

Make your first cut (Fig. 19). The photograph shows the most suitable angle for the knife. Remember to cut away from the internal corners and not to press too hard on the first cut.

The first shape is removed and the second veneer positioned under the window and taped into place. Again, choose a veneer which is easy to cut.

Cut through the window to produce the first inset piece of veneer. (Fig. 20) The following tips may help guide you to cutting success a little quicker, or even improve your existing technique.

- Have a good even light intensity over the cutting board. A counterpoise lamp with a 40 W pearl or dayglow bulb is ideal.

- If you have problems seeing fine detail, use a magnifying glass on a stand.
- When you first start cutting hold the blade 90° to the veneer. This should give good results for the vast majority of work. A tilt of about 5° away from the vertical side of the window veneer will give a closer fit especially if the shape being produced is very narrow in places. (Fig. 21).
- Unless you are using the stab method, due to the complexity of the contour, mark the bottom veneer with a very light cut first. Having ensured your first cut is correct (i.e. following the cutout closely), you can make a second slightly heavier cut but don't attempt to cut through at this stage – a heavy cut could damage the top (waster) veneer. Having marked the surface of the veneer remove it from the waster before making a further series of cuts until you can remove the selected piece. During this stage the knife must again be in the upright position.

Handling the small cut pieces can be a problem. The easiest way to cope with this is to stab them lightly with the point of the knife blade. This method has the added advantage of showing you, if it fails to pick up the veneer, that the tip of the blade has almost certainly broken off and a resharpen is necessary. It could just be the reason your cutting has deteriorated.

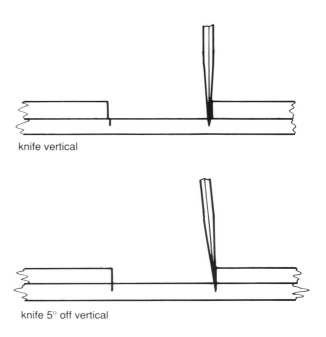

knife vertical

knife 5° off vertical

Fig. 21   Method of obtaining a more accurate witness mark when cutting through window

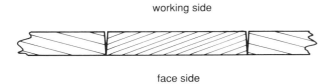

working side

face side

Fig. 22   The perfect assembled joint ready for glueing

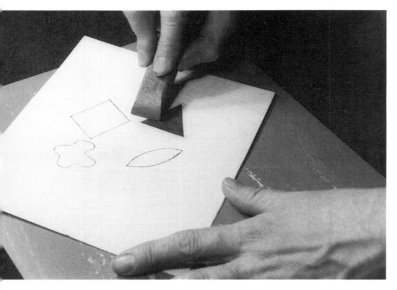

Fig. 23   Using the rubber. Note the other basic shapes useful for practice

Fig. 24   The finished result – from the face side

Fit the cut piece into the window. In theory the cut shape should fit from either back or front equally easily but in practice it is often better to lay the cut piece on the cutting mat and place the waster over it, assembling from the underside (the face side).

The surfaces *must* be flush, as shown in Fig. 22. It is not unusual to see first attempts which overlap at the edges but don't be tempted to simply press them down hard with the rubber to squash them together.

Hold the assembled sheet up to the light to see if there are any gaps. Doing this tends to exaggerate any imperfections so don't be too disheartened if you see some daylight but if the blade of the knife will easily slip through the joint then the gap is really too great. If the joint is very poor just try again. Pieces larger than about 50 mm (2 in.) in any direction may have to be held into the waster using veneer tape. This should be applied as sparingly as possible to the *face* side of the veneer. As long as you keep the amount of tape used to a minimum you can leave it until the veneer is glued on to its mounting board.

When you are satisfied that the fit is adequate, apply a little PVA glue over the joint on the working side, the side which should be face up during all the operations so far. Don't use too much glue and rub it into the joint with a fingertip to fill the small gap between the veneers.

Now use the rubber to ensure the veneers are flat and level and to help force the glue down into the veneer joint (Fig. 23). With the slight swelling of the wood due to the absorption of the glue, the rubber encourages the veneer to spread a little, filling any slight gaps. A second inspection of the joint by holding it up to the light should confirm a much better fit.

Should you still have a gap do not add extra glue; it will not help. All you will achieve is rather soggy veneer which will tend to buckle and make the edge-to-edge joint impossible to achieve. A build-up of glue on the back face is also to be avoided. If gaps still exist which are larger than you find acceptable simply cut a second or even a third piece through the window until one meets your standard.

Viewed from the face side the joint should look clean and sharp (Fig. 24).

Make further practice cuts, of increasing complexity as you become proficient in the simple shapes. Cutting out windows which cut into previously cut and glued pieces, is also good practice and indicates how this process is used to maintain grain pattern as an area disappears and reappears from behind a foreground feature. It also helps to illustrate how fine complex shapes can be produced by cutting in large areas which are then cut away to leave a thin strip.

If you can master a series of basic cut shapes as illustrated in Fig. 23, you should be able to cope very well with your first picture.

5

Further Useful Techniques

This chapter looks at a number of techniques which can be employed to improve further your standard of marquetry and parquetry. All are used in one form or another in the projects detailed in Chapter 9.

SAND SHADING

Sand shading is used mainly to darken areas of the veneer to give an illusion of depth. A darkened edge to a veneer gives the impression that it is passing behind the adjacent veneer. This can be used to good effect in many pictures, and also in parquetry as seen in the trellis design described in Chapter 6 and shown in Figs 33 (p. 47) and 47 (p. 54). It can also be used to give a rounded appearance to a surface which would otherwise look very flat by giving the hint of a shadow on both sides of the surface. It is better to use a veneer with a natural colour graduation to give this effect but finding such pieces is often difficult and sometimes impossible and shading is the only alternative. Shadows, in general, are best cut in with a darker shade of veneer rather than sand shaded because in bright light conditions the edge of the shadow is a hard line not the gradual darkening of shading.

It would be difficult to find a picture in marquetry that would not benefit by at least a touch or two of sand shading. Successfully shaded work does not appear at first glance to have been shaded at all: if you can see an obvious burn at the edge of a piece of veneer then it is probably overdone. The art is to make the shading subtle and to use it sparingly.

Fig. 25   Sand shading by laying the veneer on the hot sand

What you will need
- A heater and heating tray (see Chapter 3).
- Sand. Any washed, fine sand will do but birdcage sand is a safe bet.
- A pair of long tweezers or long-nosed pliers.
- An old teaspoon, pinched at the front to form a funnel.

There are three main ways of tackling the shading:
- Immersing the cut pieces in or laying them on the sand. This method probably gives greatest control over the shading. Best results may be achieved if the piece to be shaded is laid on the sand (Fig. 25) rather than immersed in it. If you are trying for a more dramatic effect plunge the veneer into the sand but make sure you do not touch the bottom of the dish as this will result in the immediate incineration of your painstakingly cut piece. Trial and error with scrap pieces of veneer is the finest

way of learning this technique, especially of determining the time that a particular veneer will need for the depth of shading required. As a guide, a count of one to six will usually be enough depending on the wood, temperature of the sand and effect required.

For very small pieces and fine edge work you should consider using just a spoonful of hot sand so that you have more control. Note: the veneer will not shade at the point where it is being held with the tweezers.

- Pouring the hot sand on to the cut piece from a spoon (Fig. 26). Hold the piece of veneer with tweezers, and pour the sand on to the area to be shaded, tipping it off again after a few seconds. Keep repeating this procedure on both sides of the piece of veneer until you have the effect you want. This method is less controllable than dipping into sand but has the advantage that the shading can be produced over any part of the veneer piece rather than just on the edge. Don't try to shade too large an area using this method; consider cutting in a deeper shade of veneer instead.

- Scorching the veneer sheet, by either of the above methods, before cutting, and then manoeuvring the veneer under the window of the waster to get the best effect from the shading. This method can be useful if you find that the veneer is shrinking a lot when you do the sand shading. The difficulty can be in getting an equal shading on both sides of the veneer so that you achieve the same effect on the face side as on the cutting side. (Remember, this is the back of the piece of marquetry.)

All these methods have their drawbacks. For instance, there will always be some shrinkage in the veneer as the natural moisture dries out. This can be overcome by damping the veneer immediately after shading and then placing it under a flat weight for some minutes before fitting it into the picture. Also, a small amount of shrinkage is usually corrected by rubbing in the PVA adhesive a little more vigorously than normal. Shrinkage, warping and burning are all at their worst when using the pouring method.

Remember to brush off all particles of sand from the veneer and the cutting board, as any left will seriously damage the health of your cutting blade.

Fig. 26 Sand shading by dropping the hot sand onto the veneer

Fig. 27 Repair of veneer using zig-zag cut. The inset is not quite in place, to show up the joint

Any veneer with glue on the surface, possibly rubbed into the surface to make it easier to cut, will cause a problem if you attempt to shade it. The glue, being a thermo-plastic, will soften and become coated with sand.

Some veneers will shade easier than others, some will shrink more and some will warp. Most of the light, soft woods shade well, the hardwoods with greater difficulty. Harewood does not go a darker grey, it turns brown. By contrast, green magnolia will go a darker shade of green if gently heated on the surface of the sand. *Never* attempt to shade wet veneer.

Apple, ash, aspen, birch, chestnut, maple, willow, obeche, pear, sycamore and yew are among those veneers on which you should try shading first. Experimenting is the only sure way of acquiring skill in this process.

FINE TOOTH CUTTING

This method of cutting owes its existence entirely to the veneer preparing trade. Toothing together joints (Fig. 27) is the only way to join two pieces of veneer across the grain (end to end) without it being noticeable when finished and polished. It can serve the same purpose in marquetry; it enables the marquetarian to blend together different shades without using a straight knife cut across the grain, which cannot always be hidden. It also saves time looking for that piece of veneer that changes shade along the grain, a rare bird in the veneer world especially if you require a change in colour also.

First of all it is essential for this type of work to have a knife with a long cutting edge protruding from the handle, for instance an 'Xacto' craft knife, or a Swan Morton scalpel No. 3 with a No. 10a or No. 11 blade. It also helps to round off the rather harsh bevel line on the blade to blend in the two facets on the blade. You do this by laying the blade flat down on a fine oilstone or silicon carbide paper (240 – 320 grade) rubbing it, tilting the blade slightly towards the bevel. This also helps to thin the blade as a whole, which keeps the cuts nice and fine, something not always possible with a fresh blade. With the Xacto blades we use this method when starting a new blade whether using the zig-zag cutting technique or ordinary marquetry methods.

The actual spear points are not drawn on to the original outline drawing but are added to the waster after the outline drawing has been transferred to the waster using carbon paper. Looking at the design you are copying and using some imagination, sketch the spear points or zig-zag lines on to the waster where changes in shade are required.

The drawing in Fig. 28 is taken from a detail of a flower head (*Gazania*) which was applied to the base of a dressing-table mirror (Fig. 170, p. 132, shows a detail of the base). Petal 1 shows the desired colour separation: tips in sycamore, the middle in avodire, with rosa peroba at the base.

The first step is to insert a piece of sycamore, using the window method, into the tip of the petal, bringing it down beyond any of the points you are going to cut (see petal 2). When using this process the grain must always be in line with the intended spears, in this case along the length of the petal. You may now draw the points on the sycamore (see also petal 2), but make sure that you do not make them all regular; some should be long and some short and after some practice it is a good idea to try to curve them a little to follow the curve of the petal. Petal 3 shows an example of the wrong way to mark out and cut the points.

The next step is to cut out the window marked X in petal 4 between the end of the sycamore and the line beyond the end points on the avodire. Place the avodire beneath the window and hold it in place with draughting tape. In this case the object of the window is mainly to ensure that the grain of the avodire is aligned correctly. Now cut through the points in the sycamore until the avodire below is marked as well – veneer tape on the surface of the avodire veneer may make it easier to see the fine cut marks made. The actual cutting method to employ at this stage is as follows:

Fig. 28 Zig-zag or spear cutting as applied to flowers on the dressing table mirror (p. 132)

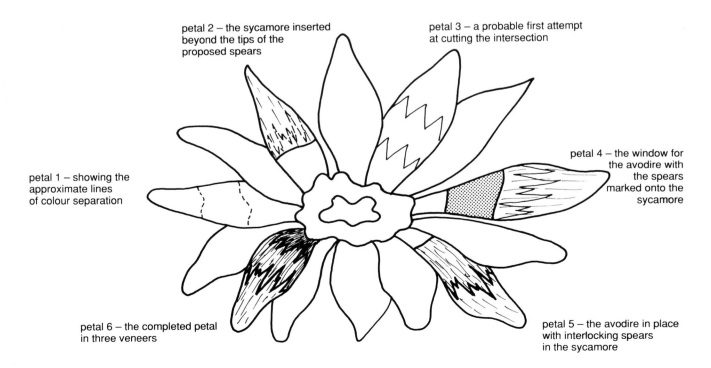

petal 2 – the sycamore inserted beyond the tips of the proposed spears

petal 3 – a probable first attempt at cutting the intersection

petal 1 – showing the approximate lines of colour separation

petal 4 – the window for the avodire with the spears marked onto the sycamore

petal 6 – the completed petal in three veneers

petal 5 – the avodire in place with interlocking spears in the sycamore

Fig. 29 Inserting the knife at the base of the spear point

Fig. 30 Bringing the blade down and along the cutting line. Note the changed angle of the blade

1. Insert the knife point into the base of the spear point (Fig. 29).

2. Bring the blade down so that more of the blade is cutting and at the same time draw the blade towards the tip of the spear (Fig. 30).

3. Repeat the process, always working from the base to the tip of the spear; and if possible cutting through the sycamore into the avodire in a single stroke.

The rest of the window is now scribed round on to the avodire which, once completed, can be removed from the back of the waster. To cut the points on the avodire turn the veneer round so the spikes are towards you and then cut through the veneer starting at the base of the points and cutting down through the points into the waste part of the veneer. The cutting action is the same as for cutting the points.

An alternative is to cut the spears in the sycamore first and then, in the traditional window method, place the avodire under the window and, using the method described above, to draw the knife from the base to the tip of the sycamore spears while holding it at a low angle and following the sides of the spear. The problem in cutting like this is that the points tend to sway slightly away from the knife edge at the thin end of the point and will require the aid of a fingernail to steady it and keep it in place as you cut (see Fig. 31)

Now offer the pair of zig-zag spears to one another, pushing them together from the straight cut end and if you find they don't quite engage run the

Fig. 31 Using the window method to cut the spears. The fingernail holds the cut veneer steady

point of the knife down the cuts to ease them slightly. When pushing them together place a finger lightly on the points to prevent them from overlapping and splintering. Because the points are so fine, should they fail to interlock exactly, any gaps will only be minute and will probably disappear when adhesive has been rubbed into the surface.

Many different veneers can be zig-zag cut together using this method to produce a blending of colour and tone ideal for a wide range of subject matters, including flowers, birds, portraits, drapery and clothing. You can also use sand shading in conjunction with zig-zag cutting to create a realistic three-dimensional effect, although you have to be extra careful lest the slender points end up as charcoal!

FRAGMENTATION

The representation in marquetry of trees, bushes and hedgerows can be difficult as we do not possess veneers which can easily depict the foliage of these plants. We can overcome the problem of trees and hedgerows as seen in the distance by using light-coloured burrs (walnut, treated ash, masur birch, harewood, etc.) provided we cut the veneers in irregular shapes and we use burrs with plenty of knots and twirls.

A tree to the foreground of a picture, set just inside the border, the trunk up one side with the branches and leaves arching over the skyline to create a frame through which we view the scene beyond, can prove an easier task as branches, twigs and leaves can all be cut individually.

A tree which appears between the foreground and the horizon creates the greatest problems for the marquetarian. The usual way of depicting these is to cut jigsaw-type shapes, using varous burrs for the foliage, and leaving spaces through which the sky or background can be seen and in which branches and twigs can be introduced. Careful choice of burrs and shapes, possibly with some sand shading for shadow effect, plus care in cutting trunks and branches can produce a realistic effect but it is all too easy to end up with what look like rows of bedgraggled old cabbages or toffee apples on sticks! An example of this technique appears in our step-by-step picture as seen in the second colour section, the small tree being specifically introduced into the picture to show what a problem they can be.

An alternative, although not a solution, is fragmentation, which is the use of chopped-up, tiny particles of veneers which are forced, with glue, into our window space.

To make the fragments:
First cut thin strips of veneer, not more than 0.75 mm (^{1}/32 in.) wide, either with or across the grain.

If you cut along the grain use a long-bladed knife as this will not catch and follow the fibres as would the pointed knife normally used in marquetry. Cut plenty of strips and then roll them together and, using the long-bladed knife, chop them across the

grain about every 0.75 mm (^{1}/32 in.) to produce the fragments. In practice it is not as easy a process as it sounds! The small chips tend to fly everywhere. If you cut your strips across the grain using a pointed knife it is not difficult with most woods afterwards to break up the strips between finger and thumb into the tiny pieces required.

Alternatively, pay a visit to your local model shop and buy some of the small packets of dyed sawdust sold for the model railways scenery, though we find this material is a little too fine.

The appeal of fragmentation is that you can mix green-dyed veneers with natural shades in various proportions to tone down the colour and give a very realistic leaf effect. An enthusiast of this method will collect different shades in small bottles in readiness.

For our sample tree, as shown in Fig. 32, we cut three different shades of green and a dark American walnut into fragments and stored each separately.

To apply the fragments:
The first step is to cut the window in the normal way restricting its size to approximately a diameter of 10 mm (^{1}/2 in.). Then, stick veneer tape over the hole on the front of the work, the reverse side to that we are working.

Spread PVA adhesive all over the taped area, making sure that the edges of the window are covered, then sprinkle small amounts of the different coloured fragments into the recess formed by the window to give the required effect of colour, light and shade. Lightly tamp them down with the flat end of the knife or a spoon; this can sometimes prove a bit messy as some of the fragments stick to your tools. Make sure you have plenty of the fragments in the window, even to the point of having a small heap, but don't let too many fragments overlap it, and work them in with the tip of your knife to ensure that the edges are tightly packed.

You now need to compact this down flat. Cover both sides of the veneer with polythene to prevent sticking and clamp it between two pieces of flat scrap wood, applying pressure with a G clamp. In the case of larger pieces of work a press could be used.

The tree should be made up in small areas leaving patches of sky waster into which small branches can be cut.

Fragmentation should be restricted to small areas and left to the last operation on the picture before laying as these areas tend to be rather flimsy. It is a technique best used sparingly.

Fig. 32 Fragments of veneer being placed into the window prior to pressing

REVERSE WINDOW CUTTING

This technique uses the same skills as the window method but in a rather different order. It is used where you wish to complete the marquetry of small pieces having a simple outline on a separate waster sheet, and insert them into a part-completed design. A typical example of the application of this technique can be seen on the ivy-covered box in Fig. 33. The method used was as follows:

1. The trellis design was completed on the developed box shape by the process described in Chapter 6.

2. On a suitable waster material (sap walnut is ideal) a number of ivy leaves of various sizes were drawn and completed, in terms of marquetry.

3. A selected leaf was cut, with care, from the waster and laid on the trellis and moved about to establish its best position.

Fig. 33 An example of work carried out by reverse window cutting in which the completed ivy leaves were cut into the previously prepared trellis work

Fig. 34 The butterfly (right) is cut from the old waster (bottom left) which in turn is placed over the new waster and marked through the window with the knife (centre)

4. Rather than cut round the leaf, which could result in an oversize aperture, the hole from which the leaf was cut was placed in the desired position. This was now used as a window through which the leaf shape could be cut to produce an aperture which could not be oversize; indeed, whether as a result of luck or skill a perfect fit for the leaf was the result!

On this design all the leaves were cut in by reverse window cutting, the trail of the ivy having been predetermined. The butterflies on the base of the Chinese checkers board seen in Fig. 34 were also put in by this method. It is especially useful when you want a new subject in a picture, and do not wish to disturb the main design. A successful attempt can be cut in when it is almost complete.

◆6◆

Parquetry

Parquetry is the collective name given to precision-cut pieces of veneer arranged into geometric patterns similar to mosaics. Parquetry has probably been with us far longer than marquetry as patterns of this nature were found decorating boxes and other artifacts in several of the Egyptian pharaohs' tombs. Much later the Dutch and French cabinet-makers of the sixteenth and seventeenth centuries used it to great effect.

Parquetry designs are ideal for use where a large area is to be veneered. Some of the standard designs can also be very happily incorporated into small applied pieces, as seen in Chapter 9. The ivy leaf jewel box, Fig. 111 (p. 99), and the tea caddy, (second colour section), use the trellis-work pattern and also include pictorial marquetry, as does the backgammon playing box, Fig. 153 (p. 122), which is on the same principle but with a more intricately worked design. Louis cube patterns can be seen to good effect on the small weed pot, Fig. 43 (p. 53), and on the small sample piece, Fig. 42 (p. 53). None of the examples of applied marquetry show the lattice-work design; this can only be seen on the sample piece shown in Fig. 39 (p. 51). It is one of the more simple techniques being similar to that used to produce chess boards, which we cover in Chapter 9. Parquetry designs can be used without the addition of any marquetry to produce a flat mosaic-type surface.

A few things have to be considered before we proceed with our work. It is sometimes better to make up the parquetry panels first and then design the rest of the woodwork (eg. box, door or lid) around the finished parquetry pieces, to avoid a great deal of time-consuming measuring and calculating.

Next thing to consider is the type of veneer to be used. For most parquetry patterns we use veneers with what we term a lustrous grain. This means that the veneers are usually quarter cut with an interlocking grain (straight, with the grain running first from the right and then from the left, usually in narrow stripes). These veneers, when opened up book-fashion, usually shade when polished because when the veneer is cut from the log the underside of the leaf being parted from the log usually suffers some fibre break-up. This can be compared with the face side of the next leaf which is flat cut and does not have to contend with the knife bevel (Fig. 35). Ideal veneers for Louis cubes and lattice-work designs would be sapele, mahogany, African walnut, avodire, sycamore, pear, makore and satinwood, most of which have a narrow pencil stripe, and are highly lustrous, reflecting well when polished.

Louis cubes and lattice designs are at their best when used on vertical surfaces such as doors and

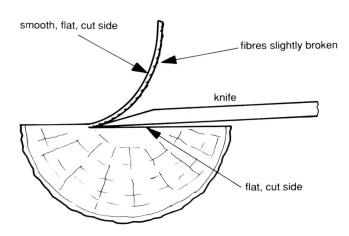

Fig. 35   Veneer cutting which results in a change in texture and shading, even when polished

sides of boxes. They rarely have the same effect on the horizontal, say on a table-top.

Lattice work is best kept to one veneer (ie. African walnut or sapele) whereas Louis cubes should be constructed from three veneers which are slightly different in colour (e.g. sapele, pear and sycamore, or African walnut, afrormosia and avodire).

LATTICE WORK

After choosing your veneers the next essential is to get a good straight edge – in hardwood or preferably metal – about 375 mm (15 in.) long, which is the same width along its entire length, this width to be that of the lattice work strips.

Method

1. Cut some of the leaves of veneer into strips down the length of the grain, 350 mm (14 in.) long

Fig. 37 Alternating layout of straight/angled cut strips ready for taping together

or longer if possible. Use a long-bladed knife for this job, not a pointed scalpel as this will tend to catch on the grain which may result in a ragged edge which follows the grain rather than the straight edge. Gauge the width of these strips from the width of the straight edge or by using a jig similar to that shown in Fig. 62 (p.66), which is used to cut border strips. These strips will form the long grain pieces of the pattern.

2. Several leaves now have to be joined together edge to edge to produce the angled grain strips. Start by cutting a straight edge along both sides of the pieces of veneer, taking off as little as possible. Lay these strips side by side as in Fig. 36, staggering them at approximately the angle you intend to cut across to avoid wastage. Then tape them together, edge to edge, with veneer tape. Make sure that the length of the proposed angled cut is about the same as that of the straight-grained strips.

3. The next step is to cut the angled strips, again using the straight edge width or jig to obtain the same width as that of the straight-grained pieces. Any angle will do, but about 45° produces the best-proportioned lattice. Cut as many strips as possible from each sheet, this time using the pointed scalpel which will cut across the grain more easily than the long-bladed knife.

4. When you have cut all the strips lay them out side by side, straight and angled grain strips alternately, the angled grain strips always laying in the same direction, as shown in Fig. 37. Again arrange the strips to minimize the wastage in veneer,

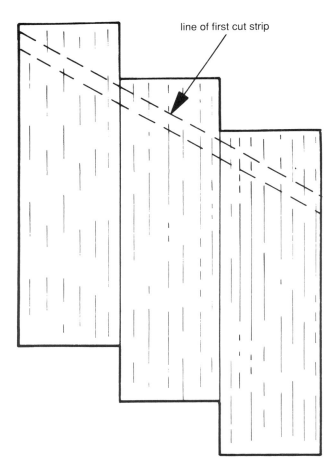

line of first cut strip

Fig. 36 Sheets taped edge to edge to avoid waste veneer

see Fig. 38. Tape together; the face side of the veneer will now be completely covered in white tape.

5. When the panel of alternating strips is complete again use the straight edge or the jig to cut it into a further set of strips at approximately the same angle and exactly the same width as the previous strips. You should end up with a strip of diamonds, with their grain directions alternating, taped together.

6. Now lay these as cut but staggered by one row in a similar manner to the chess board construction in Chapter 9, and tape them together. The initial taping can be done, with draughting tape, on the cutting side so you can see to make sure that all the small joints line up correctly, otherwise the lattice work will look more like crazy paving. Any inaccuracy in cutting will also show up at this stage. Yet again, tape the joints with veneer tape on the face side (this mean two layers of tape which will

Fig. 39   A small sample of the Lattice design showing how it can be cut to give better coverage of the required area

have to be removed after mounting). The self-adhesive tape can now be removed from the cutting side.

The whole operation may sound long and drawn out, but a couple of hours should produce a useful size panel to be cut to your individual requirements. Fig. 39 shows a possible readjustment of the made-up block which may give a more suitable shape for covering your required area. This method will prove far more reliable than cutting the diamond pieces individually and trying to fit them together one piece at a time.

LOUIS CUBES

Unlike the lattice-work pattern, which can look very flat, Louis cubes create an optical illusion of a third dimension. Although the shapes are almost identical the construction has to be tackled in a completely different way.

The process involves cutting a large number of identical diamond shapes and to do this you must construct a simple cutting jig as shown in Fig. 40. First you require a stiff vinyl-covered cutting board about 300 mm (12 in.) square as the base. To this screw a strip of hardwood about 12 mm ($^1/_2$ in.) square parallel to one edge and another at an angle of exactly 60° to the first.

As for lattice work you need a hardwood straight

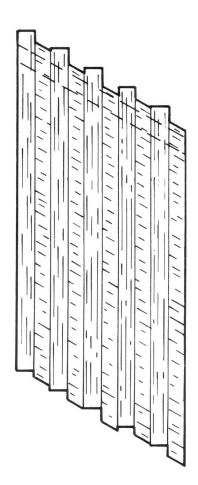

Fig. 38   Assemble straight and angle cut veneer arranged to reduce wastage at ends

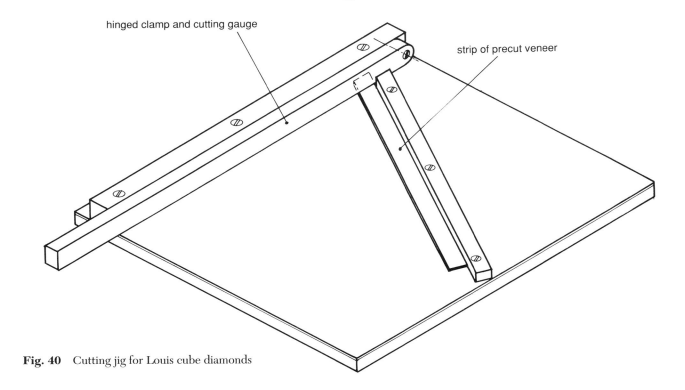

hinged clamp and cutting gauge

strip of precut veneer

Fig. 40 Cutting jig for Louis cube diamonds

edge to cut the strips which will eventually form the diamonds; it must therefore be the width of the diamond required and perfectly parallel. We have found that diamonds look best between 6 and 25 mm (^{1}/4–1 in.) wide – any bigger and the cubes lose their three-dimensional effect.

Method

1. Using the straight edge cut a number of strips along the length of the grain of your veneer with a long-bladed knife. Use three different types of veneer or three differing shades of the same veneer and be sure to cut more than sufficient.

2. When you have done this, take your hardwood straight edge and carefully hinge it with a screw to the strip which is fixed parallel to the edge of your cutting board in such a way that it can be lifted up and brought down to act as a clamp on the veneer strip as shown in Fig. 40.

3. Take one of the veneer strips and hold it against the angled hardwood template, sliding it down to butt up to the parallel piece (with the hinged straight edge raised). Lower the straight edge so that it becomes a clamp, holding the strip of veneer tightly in place. Cut the strip along the straight edge to produce the first angled end. Lift this clamp up and clear the scrap piece from the cutting board. You should now have an angled cut at the end of the strip; slide this down the angled

template strip to the parallel strip where the angles should coincide. Bring the hinged clamp down and make another cut: you have your first diamond!

4. Repeat this procedure for the whole length of the veneer strip until it is reduced to an unmanageable length. Continue with the next strip. This way you can produce diamonds quite quickly once you have mastered the technique but accuracy and not speed must be foremost in your mind otherwise the diamonds will not fit snugly together.

Note: Before cutting the strips into diamonds it may be an idea to draw a line down the length of the grain as this will help to locate the diamonds in their correct grain direction when re-assembling them.

5. The cubes can be built up on strips of masking tape, adhesive side up, held taut across a board Fig. 41), but a better material has proved to be the self adhesive polythene film used to cover books (sold at nearly all stationery and DIY shops). When pinned out adhesive side up this gives a large area which will hold the veneers together during the laying out of the cubes.

You now have a large collection of diamonds in the three shades: pick them up one by one on the tip of your knife and place in order on to the sticky plastic film (Fig. 41). Make sure that the grain of each different veneer runs in its correct direction and that this continues concurrently through all the cubes in the overall pattern as shown in Fig. 42. This

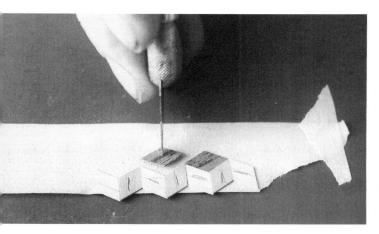

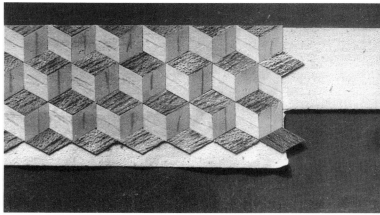

Fig. 41 Assembling the diamond faces of the cubes using the sticky tape

Fig. 42 A sample of the assembled cubes still on the tape. The lines drawn on the face help assembly

is where the pencil line indicating the direction of grain makes life easier. If you do not follow this rule the shading will differ slightly for the same veneer and the illusion of three-dimensional cubes will lose some of its effect.

When you have completed your pattern stick gummed tape (veneer tape) across the face side and remove the plastic film as this may prove inadequate to hold the veneer pieces together if they are to be used on anything other than a flat surface. A sample of the applied cubes can be seen in the detail of the weed pot shown in Fig. 43.

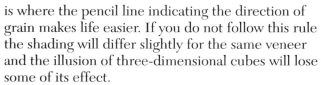
TRELLIS WORK

The trellis works very well in applied marquetry as backgrounds and borders for a range of subjects, especially to foliage and flowers which naturally grow on this type of structure. It is also useful to fill in areas where nothing else is specifically required but you want some sort of embellishment.

For the background it is best to choose a dark veneer which cuts well, especially if further detail is to be added. A walnut burr is a good choice. The trellis itself must be in a light veneer with a straight grain and easy to cut and sand shade, Horse chestnut is a most suitable wood although maple or sycamore would also be satisfactory. As accuracy is of major importance, the design is best drawn straight on to the veneer after initial designs have been produced.

Method

1. Sand shading is used to give the impression of woven trellis work. To ensure that the cutting and

sand shading are carried out according to a pattern start by shading in pencil the areas to be shaded on at least two lines of the trellis.

2. Working in a strict sequence, cut out a line of trellis pieces in the same direction. If the veneer is brittle reduce the cutting to every other slat in the trellis. Cut the strip half-way across the slat in the opposite direction as this will reduce any chance of gaps when you cut the crossing slats.

3. The trellis slats must now be prepared. These

Fig. 43 Louis cubes applied to a turned component

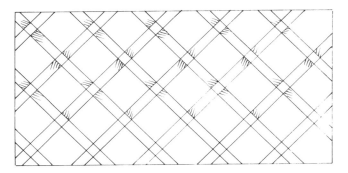

Fig. 44 Trellis production – trellis marked out and sand shaded areas marked on veneer

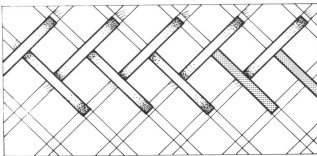

Fig. 45 Trellis production – second row of slats inserted

can either be cut to length from a stringer and then sand shaded, or a band cut to the required length, sand shaded down each side and then cut to width.

4. When the first line is glued in place you can cut the second. Working at right angles to the first line, butt up to the centre of one strip and cut through the end of another. The edges of the pattern are usually completed last. See Figs. 44–46.

Note: However you work your way through the pattern, do it systematically to avoid a patchwork effect.

Other woven patterns can be developed using this method and Fig. 47 shows a hexagonal pattern, used on the backgammon box (Fig. 153 p. 122), made in the same way.

CUTTING CIRCLES AND ELLIPSES

A marquetry inlay as the centre of a panel of veneer work is probably best done using a circle or oval inset, added when the rest of the job is complete. To produce a perfect circle or ellipse for this will be your first concern.

The first method will require access to a sanding disc machine or to an attachment on a wood-turning lathe. A plywood jig must first be made, as shown in Fig. 48. This consists of a piece of plywood about 6 mm ($\frac{1}{4}$ in.) thick and approximately square in shape of which the length of the sides is a minimum of 25 mm (1 in.) longer than the width of the sander table from disc to back. Screw a wooden batten,

Fig. 46 Trellis production – the marked-out design with the first line of trellis cut in. A few strips are also shown cut from the sand shaded band. Be careful – here the design is already fading as the glue is rubbed in

Fig. 47 Hexagonal trellis work on the backgammon box (p. 122)

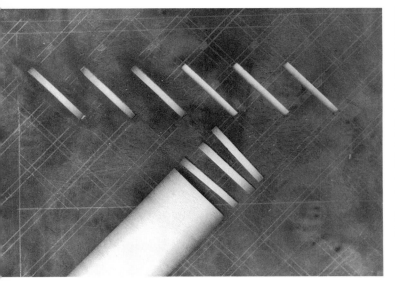

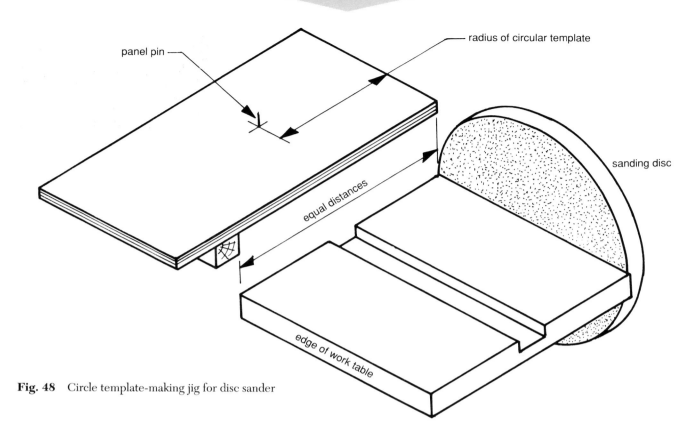

panel pin

radius of circular template

sanding disc

equal distances

edge of work table

Fig. 48 Circle template-making jig for disc sander

about 20 mm square (³/4 in.), to the underside of the plywood – this must be fitted to give the exact distance from the back edge of the sanding attachment to the face of the sanding disc itself. When placed on the work plate the jig will now advance no further than the face of the sanding disc. To set the size of the circle place a steel rule against the sanding disc and mark off the radius of the circle required on the plywood jig. At this point pierce a hole with a bradawl or drill through using a drill bit of about 1 mm (¹/32 in.) diameter. Turn the plywood jig over and knock a small panel pin through the hole. This will serve as an axle to spin the thin plywood template to form your circle.

1. Use a compass to mark out the circle on the plywood. Cut round, outside the marked line, removing the waste to leave a roughly hexagonal or octagonal shape.

2. Enlarge the compass point hole in the middle with a bradawl or small drill and place the template on the protruding panel pin on the jig – it should spin freely.

3. Now place the whole assembly on the sander

work table, turn the machine on, and push the jig towards the rotating disc until the batten stops against the edge of the work table.

4. The plywood template should now be against the sanding disc and it is important to have it positioned so that the abrasive surface is rotating down on to the template rather than pulling it up. The jig can now be clamped to the table, or you may find you can hold it with your spare hand, while the

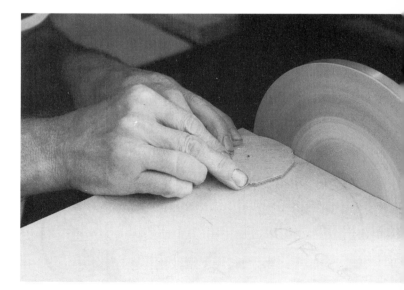

Fig. 49 Circular template being made on the disc sander using the jig shown in Fig. 6.12

other hand carefully rotates the plywood template on the pin to form a perfect circle as shown in Fig. 49.

It is now a simple matter to cut round the piece of marquetry and also to cut the circle into the background veneer using the template: the two pieces should fit perfectly.

If you want a stringer (a white or black line) around your circle this requires a slightly larger circle to be cut in the veneer. You can adapt the above method to achieve this. Cut a second plywood template using the same pivot pin but moving the jig one stringer width away from the sanding disc. You do this by placing three or four strips of waste veneer between the batten and the front of the work table to hold the jig away from the disc by the width of a stringer, which is usually about 1.5 mm (^{1}/16 in.) (see Fig. 50). You can now cut a second template using the same procedure as before. (Within limits any diameter of circle can be cut by changing the position of the pivot to the radius required, measured from the sanding disc.)

An alternative method of producing a circle requires no more than a thin strip of plywood (three ply is suitable) about 20 mm (^{3}/4 in.) wide and a little longer than the radius of the circle desired, together with a drawing pin or map pin. Push the pin through the strip to act as a pivot and measure the radius of your circle from this point to the front edge of the strip. Cut a small nick in the edge big enough to accept the blade of your knife. Now push the point

Fig. 51   Circle cutting with a beam cutter

of the pin into the veneer in which the hole is required at the centre of the circle and holding the knife upright in the nick rotate it on the veneer. Or rotate the veneer under the beam: you may find that the latter gives more control as you can concentrate on holding the knife steady and vertical (see Fig. 51).

Note: If you wish to cut a stringer into a panel in a circle or arc by the methods described above, do cut the larger circle first. The smaller circle can then be located in the same centre hole and the thickness of the stringer cut off. The method of fixing the stringer into the gap is described in Chapter 7.

There are unfortunately no easy ways to produce a perfect ellipse. You can use an elliptograph, which is a draughting instrument specifically designed to draw ellipses, to draw the outline on to thin plywood. This can then be rough cut and, finally, carefully sanded to shape, preferably on a disc sander. A cheap alternative to the elliptograph to produce reasonably accurate ellipses is the two pin, a loop of string and a pencil method. The arrangement of the equipment is shown in Fig. 52. This shows the construction of the ellipse based on its maximum and minimum axes. Approximate ellipses can be constructed using a compass to produce four arcs, as shown in Fig. 53, but the effect is not as pleasing as the true ellipse.

Some good results can be achieved using these techniques, such as the circles and ellipses on the tea caddy (second colour section).

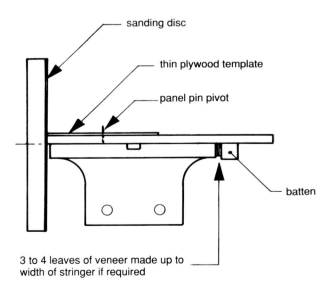

Fig. 50   Sanding disc used to cut thin plywood template for stringers

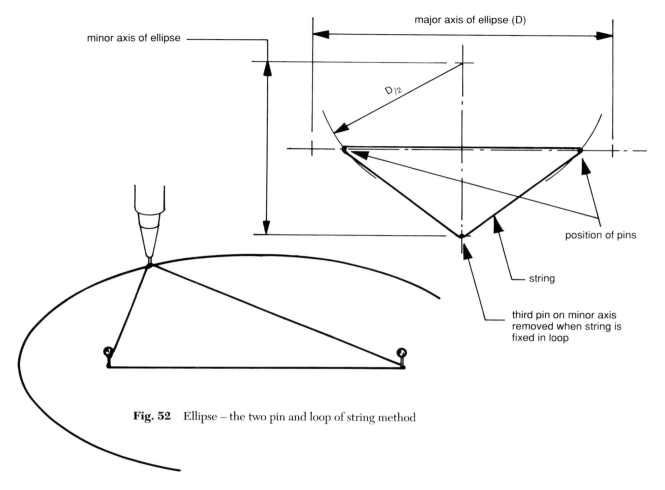

minor axis of ellipse

major axis of ellipse (D)

D/2

position of pins

string

third pin on minor axis
removed when string is
fixed in loop

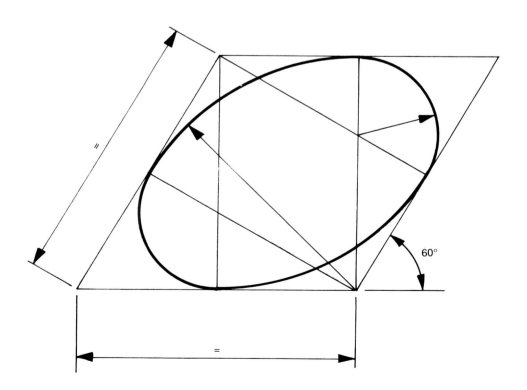

Fig. 52 Ellipse – the two pin and loop of string method

Fig. 53 Ellipse – the approximate ellipse construction from
four arcs

60°

FOUR QUARTERING

Much antique, and some modern pieces of furniture with large panels (i.e. doors, drawer fronts, decorative side or top panels) have parquetry veneers with black or white stringers, plus a border of different veneers with broken corners and mitres. Another method of covering a large area would be to use a curl mahogany, burrs, or four-quartered walnut. The two doors we shall work on to demonstrate this latter technique are being made to fit a television cabinet and the main area will be covered with a four-quartered madrona burr.

The first requirement for quartering is eight consecutively running leaves from a bundle, which will be joined up in two sets of four.

1. First line the eight leaves up, to ensure that when laid out each set of four matches up perfectly in every way. Start by laying the first leaf down on the work top and locate a prominent knot at both ends of the veneer. Lay the next leaf on top of this and line up the left-hand knot. Hold the two sheets together in place with the left hand and flip the top sheet up and down so that the right hand knots on both sheets are visible (Fig. 54). Align the two leaves and continue adding leaves, bringing all eight into perfect alignment on one feature by making all the knots appear in the same place. By applying pressure at this first point and repeating the process at another corner perfect all-round alignment can be achieved.

2. With all eight leaves lined up you can select where your first joined edge will be, ensuring that there is sufficient area left to cut the full size of panel you require. Lay a straight edge or blade of a square on the top sheet, where the first cut is to be made, and hold it in place while you make two holes along the straight edge with an awl or bradawl, held vertically, right through all eight leaves. This will give two points for cutting the individual sheets.

3. You can now make the first cut on each sheet through the points made. See Chapter 2 for advice on the straight edge to use for this sort of job.

4. When you have cut – and kept in order – all eight leaves take the first two and open them out

Fig. 54 Lining up the leaves

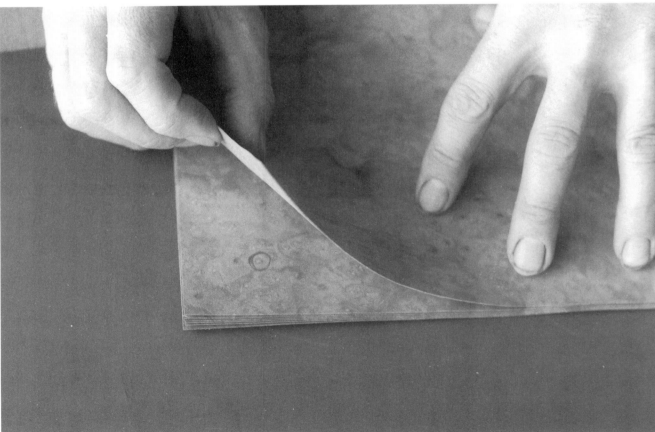

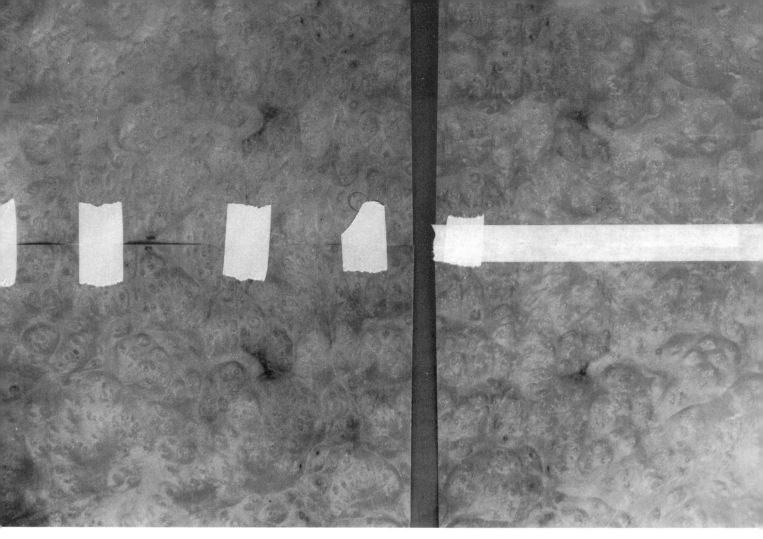

Fig. 55   Taped veneer after the matching of the two halves

open book fashion, making sure their pattern matches along the cut edge. Make a small knife nick across both leaves at the joint, turn them over, line up the nick marks and pull the joint together using masking tape.

5. The face side can now be gummed together using veneer tape and the masking tape (which was used because it is tougher, more durable and easier to remove than the thin gummed tape which becomes weak when damp) remove from the back face. Fig. 55 shows tape on the back and front as described.

6. When all eight leaves are taped up, fold them in half again with the tape hinge to the inside and stack them up into their original pile, cut edges lined up and pattern matching through the stack.

7. Using a square against the cut edge select a suitable line for the second cut edge and mark through the eight sheets with the awl at the farthest distance possible from the hinged edge. Open out the top hinged leaf flat and laying the straight edge up to the two holes make your second cut through the sheet.

8. When two pieces are cut butt them together,

face down, and with the centre joints lined up draw the sheets together as before using masking tape. Turning it face up hold the joint with gummed tape following which, again, you can remove the masking tape from the back face.

With the second pair complete you should now have two panels of four-quartered veneers which when placed side by side will match perfectly. These can now be carefully marked out from the joint line to the exact size required. Using the straight edge, trim the panels to size.

BROKEN CORNERS

The quarter round 'broken corner' as shown in Fig. 56 can be cut as follows:

1. First make two circular templates as described in Chapter 5. The larger template will cut the corner out of the four-quartered panel, and the smaller will cut the cross-banded corner piece, the difference in radii allowing for the width of the white stringer to be fitted.

Fig. 56 Prepared 'broken' corner with banding in place

2. Quarter mark the larger template with pencil lines and place it on the corner of the panel, using the pencil lines on the template as a guide. Cut round; cut all corners this way.

3. Next the white stringer and cross-veneer banding (mahogany) is taped all round using the

same technique as was used to draw the quarters of the panel together. Cut the bandings off square at the quarter circles to produce the corner similar to that shown in Fig. 56.

4. To make up the eight corner pieces, lay them in place under the corners so that the outside edges line up. Cut these in and tape them in place.

5. Now place the second, smaller circle in the corner of the panel one stringer width away from the quarter circle cut in the panel. Carefully cut the excess away from the corner veneers. Fig. 57 shows the underside of the 'broken corner' cut ready for fitting of the stringer. (The stringers are now fed into the gap as described in Chapter 7.)

When all the corners are complete turn the finished panel over, face side down, and rub PVA glue into the corner joints and stringers to secure them. The panels are now ready for the introduction of marquetry or motifs into the centres of the panels before they are mounted on to the doors.

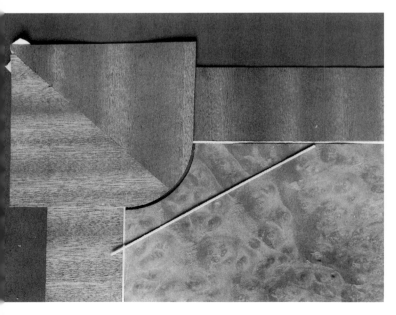

Fig. 57 The cut mitred corner ready for taping to the edge banding before the stringer is fitted

7

Mounting and Finishing

LAYING VENEERS

Applied marquetry and parquetry are very familiar sights to anyone visiting stately homes. Most of the better quality furniture has some form of veneer applied in halved or quartered configuration, with stringers and small motifs. Many pieces are covered in marquetry, and it is well worth studying the designs, cutting and shading techniques used for this work. Unfortunately the majority of the marquetry and parquetry work is in a poor state of repair, the veneers lifting, and in some cases pieces are completely missing. The nature of the veneers used, and of the base material and the type of glue that joined them all contributed to this deterioration.

The scotch glue traditionally used for woodworking and made from boiled down hooves and horns, goes brittle after a time and movement between the veneer and the base material will result in the interface of glue cracking in places. Modern veneer is very thin, about 0.7 mm (^{1}/40 in.) thick, and hence relatively flexible but the veneer used in antique furniture was hand cut, by various saw techniques, and was much thicker, about 3 mm (^{1}/8 in.), which made it quite stiff. After laying it would continue to try to warp or twist, putting the adhesive under continual stress. Finally, antique furniture is made of solid wood. Wood is porous and expands and contracts with changes in humidity (modern buildings increase this range of humidity because of the drying effect of central heating), which results in movement between the base wood and the veneers. This leads to cracks.

Modern marquetry, whether in pictures or applied to furniture, boxes, etc., uses different materials and if done correctly should give longer lasting results.

THE ADHESIVE

A range of adhesives is now available.

Scotch glue

This is still used, but mainly for woodworking joints. The problems associated with heating the glue to 120°F (50°C) in a jacketed glue pot and laying the veneer using a veneer hammer, against the relatively small advantage of being able to repair any faults in the laying, means that scotch glue is restricted in use to restoration work of antique furniture.

Gluefilm

This is the modern equivalent of scotch glue, being a very thin film of glue supplied on a backing sheet. It is really suitable only for single sheets of veneer as the glued joints (made with PVA adhesive) will soften and may allow the marquetry to fall apart when heated with an iron. But the edges of pictures, however, can be successfully stuck using this material.

Cut the sheet to size, a little larger than the veneer to be applied. In the case of an edging strip this means about 20 mm (^{5}/8 in.) longer and 5 mm (^{1}/4 in.) wider than the strip to be covered. Place the strip with its backing sheet attached, glue side down, on the edge to be veneered and touch the point of a warm domestic electric iron (the silk setting is usually about right) on to the backing sheet at about 75 mm (3 in.) intervals along the strip to hold it in position.

Now peel off the backing sheet leaving the gluefilm attached to the edge of the board. Take care to prevent the film tearing, although this type of fault can be rectified with a second layer over the damaged section. The veneer, which is also a little

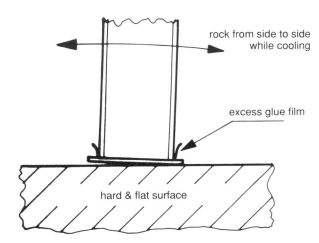

Fig. 58   Ensuring the edging veneers adhere after ironing on

larger than the surface to be covered, is then held in place while you move the warm iron slowly along its length. The main problem at this stage is holding the strip of veneer in place as the molten glue allows the veneer to slip easily if it is not firmly restrained. The excess glue will droop as the correct temperature is obtained – at this point move the iron on. Immediately the edging veneer is attached turn the board over on to a flat surface and apply pressure while rocking the board slightly to give pressure on the edges (Fig. 58) to ensure good adhesion and speed up the cooling and solidification process.

The excess veneer can be trimmed immediately. With experience you can do this with a file, but in general greater success will be achieved with the knife. Hold the veneer to be trimmed face down on to the cutting board, pressing down on the edge to be trimmed by tipping the board slightly. Place a thin-bladed knife (a Swan Morton scalpel with a no. 11 blade is ideal) hard against the edge, as shown in Fig. 59; several light cuts should trim even the most difficult veneers.

In theory the balancing veneer can be applied in the same way, but remember that the adhesive should also be similar back and front.

Contact or impact adhesives
These are air-drying thermo-plastic based glues which set as the solvent evaporates. You simply apply a film of the adhesive to the two surfaces to be glued together with the serrated spreader supplied, which gives the correct coverage of glue. Should the mounting board be very porous, such as low grade chipboard, the first coat of adhesive may largely soak into the surface which will mean a second

application. This is particularly important if you are applying veneer to the edge of a board where the area is small and the porosity greater. When the glue is almost dry (the manufacturers give recommended times, usually about ten minutes) the two surfaces are bought into contact and an instant bond is created.

This bond on contact can be a problem as the two surfaces must be aligned perfectly before they touch. Even those adhesives which claim to give some slip after contact will not do so with the fragile veneers. One solution is to place a sheet of greaseproof paper on the prepared mounting board to cover all but a thin strip at one edge. The prepared veneer is then located accurately along the edge and a little pressure applied to ensure a bond. Having aligned the surfaces the greaseproof paper can now be withdrawn from the interface and with a little luck and good craftsmanship the veneer and mounting board will locate accurately.

Next, use a small roller to apply local pressure to the mating faces. A hard rubber roller is ideal, but failing this a small wooden roller as sold for rolling down the edges of wallpaper will do (see Chapter 2). Careful rolling all over the surface should eliminate air pockets and give good adhesion. It is best to leave the marquetry face a few days before rubbing down or attempting to polish the surface as evaporation will continue, and premature sealing with the polish could cause problems at a later date.

This type of adhesive works reasonably well and requires very little equipment, but problems can occur after a relatively short time. The adhesive never sets really hard, and as a result movement can take place as it contracts. The result is cracking in the polish at the veneer joints as well as an uneven surface. Both these problems can be rectified by

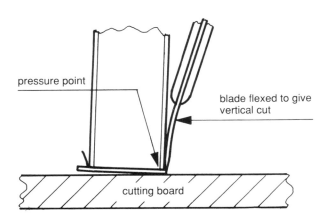

Fig. 59   Method of trimming edge

rubbing down and repolishing, but as few people actually enjoy this part of the process it may be preferable to avoid such problems if possible.

PVA woodworking adhesive

This is also an air-drying thermo-plastic, but works more by penetrating the pores of the wood to give a key when set. It is white in colour, but dries transparent, a real advantage. It is also water soluble which makes it cleaner to use and it is not expensive. To use this glue to mount veneer on to a baseboard some form of press is necessary to hold the surfaces to be bonded under pressure while the glue sets.

Only one surface need be coated with the PVA adhesive and it is far better to coat the mounting board as a coat on the veneer will soon cause it to buckle as it absorbs the water-soluble glue. The amount of adhesive is critical. Too much will cause excessive soaking of the veneer making it difficult to flatten, even in the press, and excess glue will be forced to the edges of the board giving problems of removal at a later date. Too little will result in poor adhesion in places which may not be apparent until the surface has been rubbed down flat. If you suspect air pockets, or just wish to check, then tap over the surface with your fingernail: the hollow areas which have not stuck give a dull hollow sound compared to the crisp ring of the sound bond. Careful cutting and lifting to squeeze glue into these air pockets will cause little damage if carried out before rubbing down. However, the necessity for this repair work can be avoided with care in initial glue application and good press technique.

Initial positioning of the veneer on the board is not as critical as it is with contact adhesive as the glue remains liquid for a few minutes. As the glue will penetrate right through some of the veneers, or between some of the joints which were not as good as you thought they were, it is essential to place a piece of polythene over the veneer to prevent the press plates and the mounting board becoming one large glued sandwich. A few sheets of newspaper, or similar, are also required to take up the slight variations in thickness of the veneer, the object being to get close contact between all the veneers and the mounting board (Fig. 60).

After about two to three hours remove the veneered board from the press. The glue is not fully set and therefore further work, such as rubbing down, should be delayed for a further 24 hours, but leaving the veneered board in the press for any longer will prevent the natural drying process taking place may result in fungal growth in the sandwich of damp wood. This will make small stained spots in the softer pale veneers which cannot be removed by rubbing down.

Any glazed appearance on the veneer is where the glue has penetrated through the veneer. This may be a sign that a little too much glue was used, but there is no problem as this glaze will disappear when the surface is rubbed down.

Thermo-setting adhesives

This is a two-part adhesive made up of a resin and a hardener or catalyst, usually a powder. Mixing the two parts together produces a chemical reaction

Fig. 60 Sandwich required for mounting veneers in the press

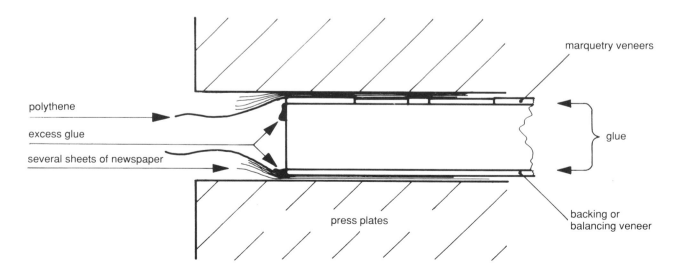

polythene

excess glue

several sheets of newspaper

press plates

marquetry veneers

glue

backing or balancing veneer

which results in the formation of a hard, brittle thermo-set which once formed cannot be softened by heat or solvents. The two parts are mixed to the manufacturer's stated proportions and applied in the same way as the PVA adhesive.

The setting time varies depending on the temperature and the type and amount of hardener used. Commercial heated presses will produce a set within minutes, but up to three days may be required with some types at low temperatures. As the hardening process does not rely on evaporation no problems exist in terms of moulds developing over long periods in the press.

The advantage of this type of adhesive is that once set no movement is likely to occur between the veneer and its mounting board. The assembly is now very stable. This material also has good gap-filling qualities which can be a considerable advantage to the not-so-practised cutter.

Disadvantages of this type of adhesive do exist. They are not cheap and can only be purchased in relatively large quantities. They also have a shelf life in the order of six to twelve months and as a result are really only viable if they can be shared, as in the case of a club. A further problem is that the excess glue squeezed out from between the mounting board and the veneer sets into very hard beads which are difficult to remove with anything other than a plane.

This adhesive is ideal for thin edge strips. The mixed adhesive is applied to the edge, the veneer strip placed in position and heat pressure applied with a domestic electric iron set to low to medium heat. The thermo-set will form in 10–20 seconds – you will see the excess glue bubbling and going white and hard, whereupon you move the iron slowly along. Don't apply too much adhesive as it has been known to penetrate the veneer and stick the iron to the edge also.

Cascamite

This is another type of thermo-setting adhesive, but the reaction is caused by the addition of water to the powdered Cascamite. After mixing it is used in the same way as PVA adhesives and gives similar results to the thermo-set but with less capacity to fill gaps caused by poor cutting. Cascamite is not cheap, but is readily available.

THE VENEER

Very little more need be said about the veneer itself (see Chapter 3) apart from the fact that differences in thickness still do exist in modern veneers and if possible any piece of work should be completed with veneers of a common thickness.

Also, due to the nature of timber, veneers are not always flat. Clamping in a press between slightly damp paper will give a temporary solution, but don't expect the veneer to remain flat for any length of time. Should you use such a veneer in a design or picture it would be as well to keep the work in a press or between boards under a weight while you are not actually working on the project.

THE MOUNTING OR BASE BOARD

For cheapness and stability nearly all modern marquetry and parquetry are mounted on to a composite board. Even plywood has the tendency to move and lift and many pieces of work produced only 15 years ago and mounted on plywood have deteriorated badly. It may be that with the modern adhesives used in producing today's plywood and in mounting the veneer the problem does not now exist, but until someone experiments, and decides after 20 years that all is well with plywood, you may prefer to stick with a more stable material.

Chipboard

Very cheap and available in a wide range of sizes and thicknesses, chipboard is used throughout the furniture trade and can be purchased ready veneered on both faces. Its main problem is its porosity, particularly at its centre, where the mixture of sawdust and adhesive is not compressed too well, and when sticking veneer or edging strips on these edges it is as well to fill the cavities before applying adhesive. It is also difficult to get a good clean, sharp edge to the board and tools used to cut or plane the board soon lose their edge due to the abrasive material which always seems to be present in with the wood particles. Any machining on this board should be carried out with tungsten carbide-tipped tools.

MDF (medium-density fibreboard)

This material is much more uniform in its structure, the fibres are finer, there is no abrasive rubbish in with the fibres and the board is much more compressed and hence much denser and stronger. You can machine it to a fine edge with saws, planes and routers with tipped blades and cutters, and it takes a stain well. It is a lot more expensive than chipboard and not so widely available, but is well worth the extra effort and expense.

PRESENTATION

Having established a few methods of laying the veneers we need to get our marquetry to a stage where it requires mounting on to its baseboard. It may appear to be putting the cart before the horse to look now at the presentation of the work which will probably involve work on the veneers before mounting, but this section assumes a knowledge of the various processes available for laying veneers.

The object of this section is to look at the use of basic borders for parquetry and marquetry and to progress to various alternative presentations and how they may affect the order of laying.

CUTTING THE PICTURE SQUARE

When cut into a waster, the picture or design is not usually cut to fit exactly into the required frame shape. There is no point in cutting the veneers at the edge to an accurate straight line which will in turn be cut again, and at times considerable difficulties can be encountered if you attempt to do so.

Method

1. The first step is to establish a true, straight horizontal or vertical line on one edge of the picture, depending on which is the most relevant to the subject matter. (Don't attempt to measure at this stage.) Trim the edge with the straight edge *on the*

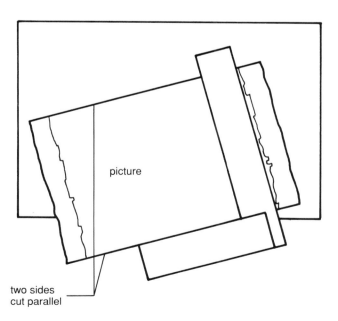

picture

two sides
cut parallel

Fig. 61   Cutting the third side square to the two cut parallel sides

design, cutting on the outside edge to avoid any slip of the knife damaging the worked veneer. Cut very lightly at first, only increasing the pressure when you are sure the knife is following a true straight line.

2. With the aid of a steel rule mark off the opposite side of the picture parallel, to a suitable dimension, and cut as before. Cut the third side using a good quality try-square. Be careful: it is easy to make a mistake when you are trying to set the try-square against the thin veneer, which must also be supported on the cutting board. The danger is to let the cutting board interfere with the try-square, and Fig. 61 shows how to avoid the problem.

3. Cut the fourth side parallel to the third using a rule and straight edge, as for side two.

You should find this method much more accurate than cutting each side square to the previous, as accumulated errors occur by that method. Measure the diagonals and check they are the same, as they should be for a true rectangle, and lay a straight edge against each side in turn to check that they are cut straight. Repeat the squaring process if an error has occurred. Don't be tempted to leave any small errors to be corrected after mounting by trimming the borders, or cutting the board to suit the shape of the picture, as the errors usually compound and become unsightly.

CUTTING STANDARD BORDERS

For this purpose we are assuming that all the borders are equal in width and hence the mitres at the corners are at 45°.

First cut the border accurately to width. Its minimum length must be the length of the longest side of the picture plus two widths of the border plus about 10 mm ($^1/_2$ in.). Should stringers be used, then twice the width of the stringers each side must also be added to the length. A reasonably accurate way of cutting veneers into border-type widths is to use a straight edge of the same width as the border.

Many special jigs have been devised for cutting parallel strips and the simplest involves a cutting board with a raised wooden straight edge. The veneer is pushed hard against the wooden edge and then the metal straight edge is placed on top, also pressed hard against the wooden edge. When cutting start with a very light cut or the grain will pull the blade. The harder you press the more the knife will tend to follow the grain. The normal marquetry knife is suitable, but a curved blade of greater thickness (hence more rigid) will help you keep to a straight line.

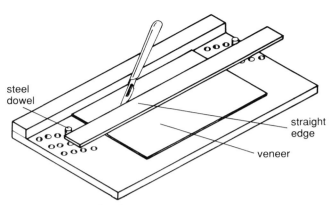

steel dowel

straight edge

veneer

Fig. 62   Cutting border veneers

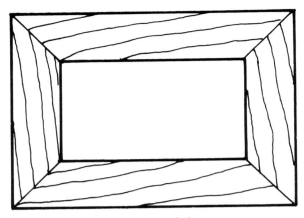

Fig. 63   Border patterns to be avoided

An alternative cutting board is shown in Fig. 62 where the width of the strips is set by a pair of steel dowels (steel because they will retain their accuracy). The position of the holes must be *very* accurate to maintain parallel strips, although the actual width is not important.

Choosing the veneer to make the border strips can be difficult as a variation in grain width or direction can give very odd effects as illustrated in Fig. 63. Sapele is one of the most popular veneers to use as its grain is very straight and uniform. If a straight grain is unobtainable in the colour you require or you choose to use the grain as a feature in some way, ensure the pattern of the grain matches on each side and top to bottom and are set as mirror images (see Figs. 64 and 65).

Thin stringers are much more difficult to cut and you would be well advised to purchase these, accurately cut by guillotine.

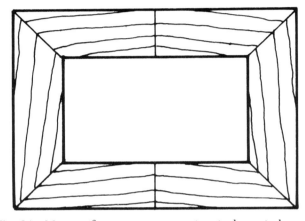

Fig. 64   More uniform arrangement using single vertical cut

ATTACHING STANDARD BORDERS

We strongly advise adding the border before gluing the marquetry to its mounting board.

1. Place the stringers (if used) and border veneer, after cutting, round the picture to ensure the effect is as required, the marquetry now being face up.

2. When you are satisfied with the arrangement, attach the borders to the marquetry/parquetry. While holding the border tight against one side attach it with a short strip of veneer tape at about 100 mm (4 in.) intervals along one side *on the face side*.

3. Assemble the other sides in the same way, working in a clockwise direction and ensuring that the corners of the border have a total overlap as shown in Fig. 66. Check again that you have got the effect you want.

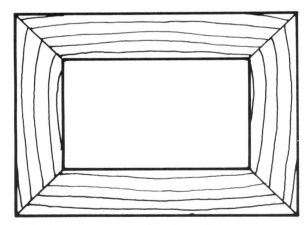

Fig. 65   Swept grain arranged to give uniform arrangement

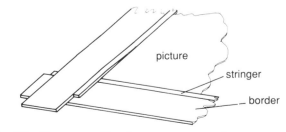

picture

stringer

border

Fig. 66   Placement of border veneer to cut mitres

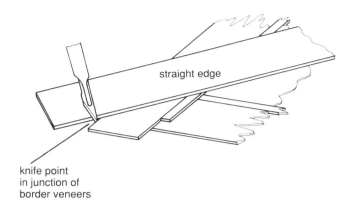

Fig. 67 Cutting mitres

4. Apply a strip of tape right along the joint between the picture and the border – but not over the corners where the borders meet.

MITRING THE CORNERS

The next stage is to cut the mitres. To do this place the marquetry on to its face, so again you are cutting from the back, and place the straight edge across the corner. The outer corner can easily be set accurately by placing the knife point into the junction of the border veneers and pushing the straight edge up to it. Only the inner corner now has to be judged, pivoting the straight edge about the tip of the knife blade on the outer corner as shown in Fig. 67. Cut through both strips, very gently at first; this should produce a very accurate mitre as long as you have been careful particularly through any hard stringers (ebony is often used to make dark stringers).

Use veneer tape on the face side to hold each corner, and rub PVA adhesive into the back face along all the border joints as further insurance against movement when it comes to laying the veneers.

Fig. 68 Mitred corner with stringers

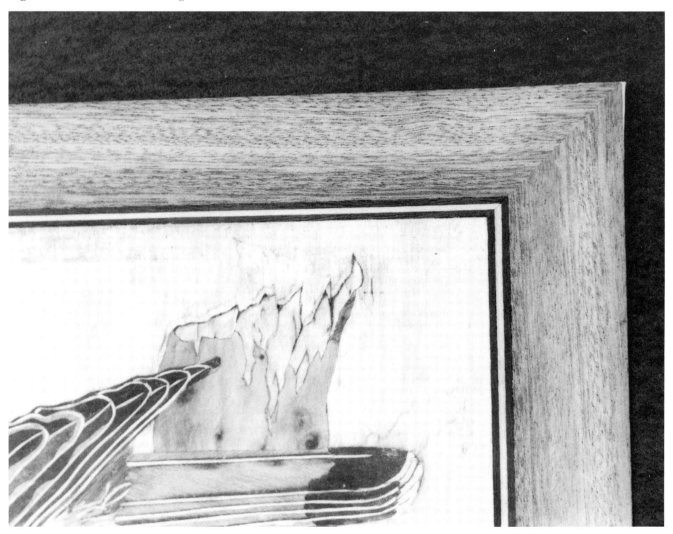

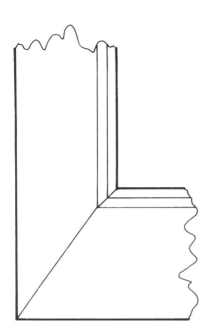

Fig. 69   Double mitres required if bottom border is wider

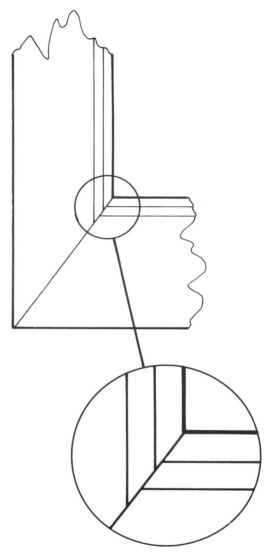

Fig. 70
Effect of a single mitre – what not to do!

This is how the mitres on the hexagonal checkers board in Figs 168 (p. 131) and 169 (p. 132) were cut. Fig. 68 shows a mitred corner with three stringers on a picture and ready for mounting.

Mitres other than 45°
Should you require a wider border at the bottom of the picture, as is normal with picture framing, then more care is required if more than a single strip of veneer is going to be used. It is easy to produce the effect shown in Fig. 70. To avoid this the stringers must be cut separately (Fig. 69), or care must be taken to ensure the stringers are proportionally wider for the base strips (Fig. 71).

SOMETHING A LITTLE SPECIAL IN BORDER DESIGN

Borders and stringers play an important part in presenting marquetry pictures and panels. They should not be added just as an afterthought but used to project pictures, add harmony and colour, and generally enhance the work. For example, a dark cross-grain border gives the appearance of depth whereas a light veneer border will throw the picture forward.

As we said earlier, borders, if possible, should be cut from the same section of four consecutive leaves and we should try to ensure that the grain is straight.

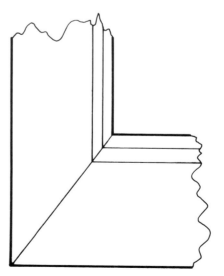

Fig. 71   Difference in stringer widths if single mitre is required – a difficult option

Fig. 72 A range of typical borders using stringers, cross cut banding and commercial bandings

If one piece has the grain at a slight angle it can made a picture look lop-sided and out of square.

It is easy just to use sapele and a white or black stringer, which we have already recommended as a basic border, but with little thought and experimentation you can produce borders of far greater interest. A range is shown in Fig. 72.

Burrs in borders

Burrs make an interesting and somewhat exotic change from sapele and other straight-grained veneers, but they must be butt jointed and matched in a similar way to that mentioned under standard borders when using figured veneers. To do this we need eight running leaves whose length must be at least half the length of the longest side when finished.

Prepare two pairs of leaves as in the first stages of four quartering described in Chapter 6.

1. Match the leaves over each other.

2. Cut one end square.

3. Open the leaves out like a book and tape them together.

4. Close the leaves and again match the cut edges and the pattern of the burrs.

5. Mark the edge of the long edge by piercing through with the awl.

6. Cut the long edges.

At this stage we effectively have a long thin four-quartered panel if you tape them together. However, instead these two pieces will eventually match at the top and bottom of the picture. To continue with the making of the border:

Fig. 73   The overall effect of the matched burr as seen in 'Venetian Alfresco'

7. Set the chosen stringer or stringers between the picture and the cut edge of the burr, ensuring that the butt joint is exactly in the centre of the base of the picture, and tape the assembly together on the face side with veneer tape.

8. Attach the same pattern of stringers to the short sides using veneer tape. You now have to work back from the corners in order to ensure that the pattern of the grain matches on all joints:

9. Cut the mitres at 45° through the stringers and bottom border.

10. In each corner in turn place a leaf of burr under the bottom/top border so that the pattern of the burr matches exactly; the mitre and the butt joint to the stringer can then be marked and cut.

11. When hinged round the corner it matches on the corner and the joints close up on the mitre and the stringer interface and can be taped in place to almost half-way up the edge.

12. With two corners on the same side complete there will be an overlap at the centre. Now cut the final butt joint at the centre of the side. This is when

you hold your breath until you find out if the figure of the burr is a perfect match!

Final trimming is straightforward using a rule and straight edge. The overall affect of a corner joint completed by this method can be seen in the

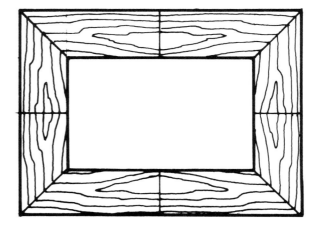

Fig. 74   Striking arrangement of borders using consecutive leaves cut to match at mitres

photograph of 'Venetian alfresco' in Fig. 73. The same principle can be effective applied to figured veneers, as shown in Fig. 74.

Machine-made banding
As well as the fine black and white stringers which can be purchased in metre lengths there is also on the market a wide selection of machine-made fancy borders which in most cases would prove almost impossible to make by hand. These also come in metre lengths and can transform what is quite a simple piece into something really special.

Cross-grain borders
The short cross-grained section of borders, an example of which can be seen in Fig. 75, are best *not* tackled by cutting into narrow cross-grained strips. These will prove to be very brittle and too easily broken into short lengths. They may also sway under

the cutting edge, resulting in a non-parallel piece which will throw the entire border and mitres out.

The best approach is to tape together the main border piece, the stringer and a wide piece of cross-grain veneer. Rub some PVA adhesive into the joints and the cross-cut veneer on the reverse side to keep it intact, and, using a steel rule and straight edge, cut the cross-cut veneer down to a narrow strip; there will be little danger of its breaking or being out of parallel. Repeat the process until you have the length of border you require. Further stringers and strips can be added to the border or between the border and picture/workpiece as it is assembled.

Note: The border is there to enhance the picture. Never should the border become overpowering; in many cases a simple single band may be more appropriate than a collection of fancy bandings, stringers and burrs, however attractive these are.

Fig. 75 Cross and angled cut border veneer

A CATALOGUE OF ERRORS

Figure 76 This border mitre shows bad matching up of the fancy banding (ringed) caused by taping the banding to the picture without checking that the pattern fits. This can be corrected by cutting down the picture to a suitable size.

Figure 77 This shows the common mistake of using two different widths of black stringer, resulting in an

overlap at the mitre and hence a slight spur (ringed). Always watch for any slight variations in width and tape matching sets of stringers together when in storage.

When one banding is straight and the other cut at a slight angle, the result is a lop-sided appearance. The diagram in Fig. 63 shows the overall effect of this fault.

Another common beginner's mistake is the knife cut over-shooting when cutting the mitre, resulting in a small cut mark in the corner which cannot be hidden. If you find this is a problem try cutting the mitre from the inside to the outer corner.

Fig. 76   Bad matching of the fancy banding

MOUNTING

Here again we are looking at the most basic form of mounting veneers which covers any veneering of flat surfaces including pictures, chess boards, trays, etc. The laying of veneers on more complex applied pieces will be covered in Chapter 9 along with the appropriate project.

For pictures the mounting board is usually cut after the marquetry is complete and the border is attached. This assists accuracy. It is much more difficult in practice to predetermine the size of a

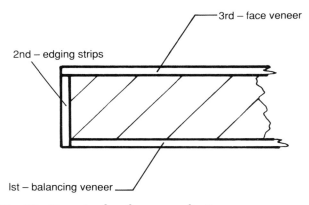

Fig. 78   Correct order of veneer application

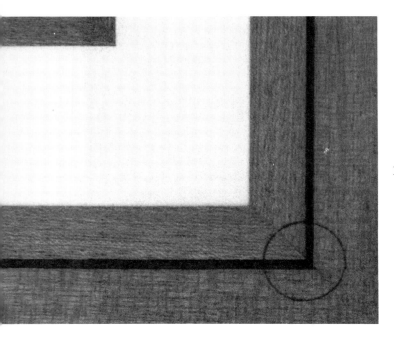

Fig. 77   Different width stringers resulting in a mismatch at the mitre

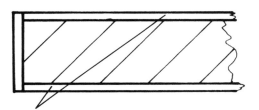

Face and balancing veneers mounted at same time

Fig. 79   Alternative order of veneer application suitable for darker veneers

trimmed picture as it is not unknown for pictures to be cut out of square at the first attempt, for straight edges to slip, and for the edge veneers to chip or have wavy edges when being cut to size using the straight edge.

The board is cut smaller than the completed piece of work to be mounted by exactly the same amount in each direction, say 3 mm ($^1/8$ in.). It must be square and the edges must be square to the face.

The correct order of application is first to glue the balancing veneer on the back, then apply the edge strips and finally the prepared face veneers (Fig. 78). This order of working is important should you be using light veneers on the border and edge. If you are using sapele or a similar darkish wood then the balancing and face veneers can be mounted together. If the operation is carried out correctly the glue line between the face and edge veneer will not show with these darker woods (Fig. 79). The various methods of laying and trimming have been dealt with earlier in this chapter under the various adhesive headings.

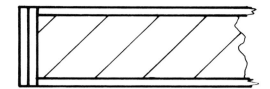

Fig. 80 Method used when dark contrast veneer used against a light face

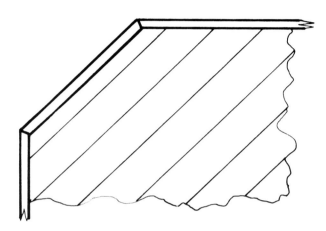

Fig. 81 Veneers butt joined where pattern is to extend around corners

ALTERNATIVE PRESENTATION

Having established how to cut mitres and successfully mounted a picture, one soon looks for alternative methods of presentation for pictures and designs. Here we look at just a few of the possibilities and from these you, no doubt, can expand and experiment to produce your own original display ideas.

NO BORDERS

The idea of a border can be discarded, particularly if the waster comes to the edge of the design all the way round. In this case two alternatives present themselves:

1. Wrap the waster round to form the edge veneer for the mounting board. In this case it is important to follow the grain direction and pattern, and the edges must be applied before the face veneer. Great care must be taken to ensure the correct positioning of the edge veneers and it may be better to use gluefilm as the edge adhesive so that you can move the veneer if necessary by reheating with the electric iron.

2. Use a contrasting veneer on the edge. In this case apply the edge veneer after the face veneer, and

to get a reasonably thick edge line use two thicknesses of veneer on the edge (Fig. 80). An ebony veneer is usually a good choice if the waster is a light veneer.

A further enhancement of this idea is the addition of stringers within the picture to form a complementary thin line to the edge veneer, or short lengths at the corners which may be further developed into a simple pattern as shown in Fig. 82.

When inserting stringers into the picture, do so before cutting to size to maintain maximum stiffness and strength while cutting the long thin cut-outs. Cut the outer side of the stringer window first, follow by the inner, to maintain stiffness for each cut. Mark the line and width of the stringers on the back of the worked veneer and do take care – there is no second chance at cutting the window unless you remove a lot of the picture. When fitting the stringers use tape on the face side to hold them in place and rub PVA adhesive into the joints on the reverse side.

MOUNTING ON A BACKING BOARD

This gives the picture a raised mount which can add interest with its extra dimension. Mount the picture

Fig. 82 Stringer developed into a corner pattern

Fig. 83 A satin finish on the picture surface, which is mounted on a thin backing board in turn mounted on a larger base board, the veneer of which has a high gloss finish

on thin, say 6 mm ($^1/_4$ in.), board with balancing veneer and edges glued on. Choose a thicker material for the backing board, about 15 mm ($^5/_8$ in.), and cut it large enough to give a reasonable border. This should be veneered on the face with something that will really set off the picture; the edges and back must also be covered. Both boards must be polished to the required finish before they are glued together in an appropriate position (see also the detail in Fig. 83).

CUTTING INTO A BACKGROUND VENEER

With this presentation neither the picture nor the mounting board is restricted in shape. Taking the basic rectangular picture, first cut it to a true rectangle and then lightly tape it, face side up, with pieces of masking tape, on to the piece of veneer which will form the border. With the aid of a straight edge make a cut following one edge of the picture and before proceeding remove the cut masking tape and use veneer tape to hold the picture and surround together. Repeat this process on each of the other three sides.

The picture is now held in its border and adhesive can be used on the under side to help hold it in place. If the frame is to be rectangular also it is a simple matter to measure the width of the border from the picture. The process of setting the picture in the border is the same as the reverse window method described in Chapter 6.

SETTING IN A STRINGER

For a circular pattern the first problem is to cut a circle in the border veneer whose radius is a stringer's width larger in radius than the picture (see Chapter 5).

The next problem is to fit the stringer into the circular gap. The stringers, especially those made from harder woods such as ebony, will resist being bent round into a curve and will tip over if not well restrained. To reduce resistance to bending make oblique cuts about two-thirds the way through from the inside edge. Figs. 84–86 show the effect of bending the stringer in the correct and incorrect directions (i.e. with the cuts to the outside).

After you have placed the circular picture face up inside the cut-out fit the first short length of stringer in the gap and tape it into position. Working round the circumference of the circle about 25 to 50 mm (1–2 in.) at a time, depending on the size of the circle, ease the stringer into place, taping as you go. With the harder and slightly wider stringers it may help to damp the veneer slightly, but if the required width exceeds about 2 mm ($^3/_{32}$ in.) then you should consider a double width of thinner stringer. On completing 360°, or at any place where a joint is required, cut the stringer obliquely – an oblique cut is far less visible than a butt joint. As in all of these processes you then rub glue into the joint on the back face. (This process is also used on the cabinet doors as described in Chapter 6.)

Dealing with an ellipse is a little more difficult and cutting the border veneer is carried out in a slightly different manner. Position the picture, cut to an ellipse, face side up in the centre of the border and tape it in place with draughting tape. Set the stringer, with oblique cuts to the inside as before, round the outside which is also taped down a short length at a time. Using the outside of the stringer as a template, then cut the border veneer. As you cut a

Fig. 84 Stringer prepared for bending with oblique cuts

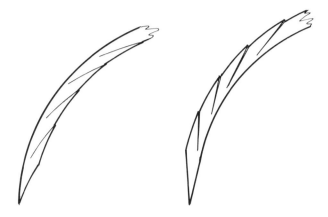

Fig. 85 Correct bend with cuts to inside

Fig. 86 Incorrect bend showing effect of opening the cut

short length, remove the draughting tape and use veneer tape to hold the picture, stringer and border together. The centre of the border will fall away as the last section is cut.

APPLYING VENEERS TO CURVED SURFACES

In the past shaped and moulded parts of furniture, boxes, clocks, etc. were all constructed of solid wood and the need to veneer these surfaces was not always paramount. Nowadays, with the very high cost and limited availability of good timber, modern furniture is largely made of composite materials (chipboard and MDF) which is veneered. Veneering of curved surfaces can be done by the amateur woodworker using contact adhesives or with one of the following methods.

THE FLEXIBLE CLAMP METHOD

This method was used to apply veneer to the bow front of the flower-covered jewellery box shown in Fig. 112 (p. 100). PVA adhesive or Cascamite could have been used and was applied to the curved surface of the box and the prepared veneer placed in position. Next a strip of polythene was placed over the veneer to prevent any glue percolating through

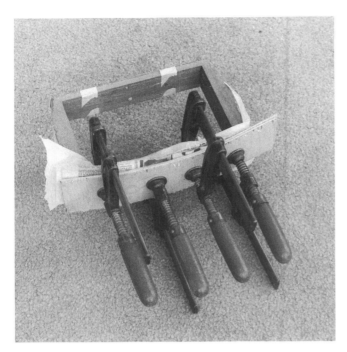

Fig. 87 The use of G-clamps and two thin sheets of plywood to glue veneer in place on the curved front of the jewellery box (see Fig. 112, p. 100).

the joints or pores of the wood and creating a joint we do not intend. This was followed by several strips of waste paper to take up any slight differences in the thickness of the veneers.

To apply pressure two pieces of 3 mm (^{1}/8 in.) plywood cut on the cross grain were used. One piece of 6 mm (^{1}/4 in.) plywood would have been far too stiff whereas two thin strips bent easily to shape, to fit exactly the box's bow front. Several strips of masking tape held the plywood together to stop any movement.

With the sandwich of box front, veneer, polythene, paper and plywood in place G-cramps were applied, starting in the middle and working down each side in turn (see Fig. 87).

Fig. 88 Clock blank cut from block board, the waste becoming the former for clamping the veneer

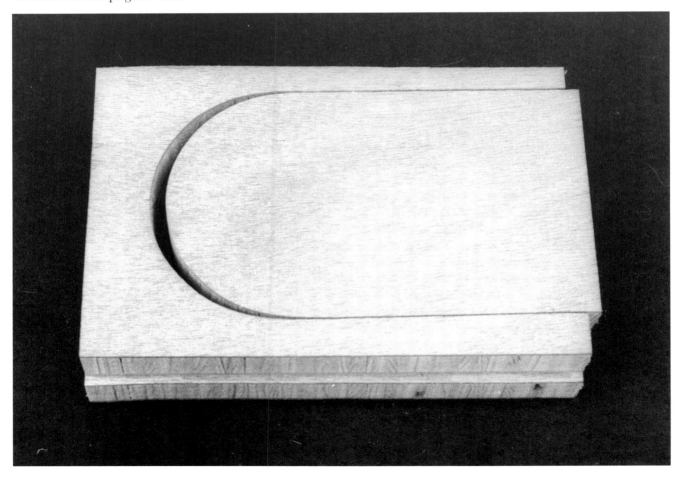

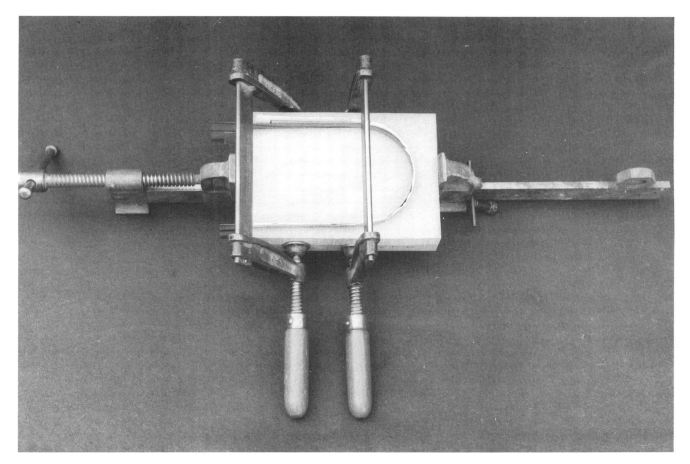

Fig. 89 Clock blank with the side face veneer glued and clamped in place using the cut waste as the former

THE MALE-FEMALE METHOD

This method requires a two part jig, one part of which is the item to be veneered, and it can apply sufficient pressure to enable more complex shapes to be veneered. Here we are going to describe how to apply it to the dome shaped clock (see second colour section).

First cut the block of material to shape on the band saw. This must be done with great care, keeping the cut very smooth, as it cannot be sanded and any deviations round the 'U' shape will show up in the finished article. Figure 88 shows the cut blank made from two thicknesses of blockboard glued together.

You now have your male/female jig, the male piece eventually to become the clock and the female later to be discarded. The 'kerf' or saw cut will be slightly wider than the thickness of the veneer. The necessary piece of polythene plus a few sheets of paper will make up that gap and give a perfect fit.

When you have applied glue to the edge (PVA or cascomite) and placed the veneer, polythene and

paper in position, push the whole assembly as far as possible gently into the female piece and use a sash clamp to tighten up top to bottom, pushing and holding it in place firmly until glue is seen escaping from the joint. G-cramps can now be used to apply pressure to the sides as shown in Fig. 89. Leave for about two hours for perfect adhesion. Remove clock blank.

Any shape which can be cut with the band saw can be veneered using this method.

PREPARATION OF THE SURFACE

Many pieces of work are let down by a poor finish due to rushing the last stages. This is a pity as even a fairly basic piece of marquetry can look impressive if finished well.

The initial task, after mounting, is to rub down the surfaces of the work until they are flat. It is essential to bring the surfaces down to a smooth, flat finish before any attempt is made to polish them. This would

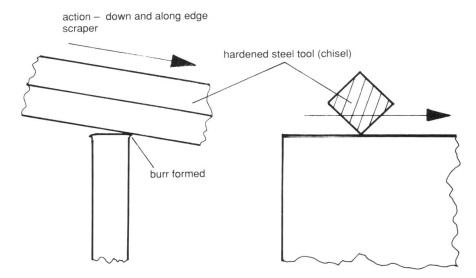

action – down and along edge
scraper

hardened steel tool (chisel)

burr formed

Fig. 90   Setting burr on the scraper

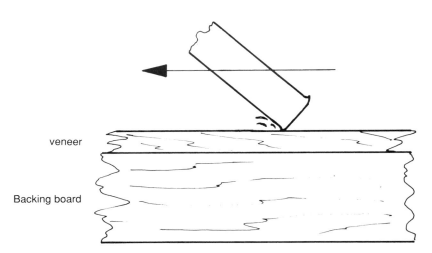

veneer

Backing board

Fig. 91   Scraper action

appear to be simple but it can cause major problems, especially if short cuts are attempted. The veneers are not the same thickness and vary considerably in hardness and hence in their resistance to abrasion. Beginners often work on the assumption that the polish, if applied thick enough, will eventually produce a flat surface, but this approach will only lead to a lot of hard work and some disappointment.

Before starting on the flattening process take any precautions necessary to prevent the spread of dark or deep coloured veneer dust (padouk, ebony, etc.) into the pores of the soft, open-grained, light woods (sycamore, maple, magnolia, etc.). This process is described in Chapter 4 under the description of paduak. Some fine pieces of work have been spoilt by ignoring the staining effect of these veneers when rubbing down and polishing.

A minor problem can exist in holding flat sheets of work (pictures, small doors, etc.) during the flattening process and various implements have been 'invented' to hold flat boards secure during this operation. One such piece of equipment is shown in Fig. 12 (p. 23) and works on the principle of wedges for clamping and movable stops to accommodate various sizes of board. In practice we have found that a square of carpet makes a good base when sanding, but the clamp shown held in a 'workmate', woodworking vice or used against a stop on the bench is worthwhile if you decide to use a cabinet-maker's scraper.

This tool requires some skill to use efficiently and effectively, particularly on marquetry or parquetry where the grain is changing in direction so often. The tool was developed as a means of smoothing down areas of timber by working it along the grain, and is not so effective when working across the grain. Depending on the timber, cross grain working can tear out the surface fibres of the wood and in marquetry is capable of tearing the veneer through to the base board. We do not use the scraper as a tool for marquetry and would not recommend it for those reasons: however, if you do want to experiment, this is how to use it.

The scraper is a thin hardened and tempered steel plate, and the cutting is done with a burr thrown up on the straight edge. This is achieved in two stages. First, hone the edge flat, straight and square using an oil stone. Then form the burr using a hardened steel tool with an angled edge, such as the edge of a wood chisel, by drawing it across and along the scraper edge at a slight angle to the prepared square edge (see Fig. 96). Hold the scraper in two hands, thumbs at the centre and fingers pulling back against the forward pressure of the thumbs, so that the scraper is firm and has a slight bow. Angling the scraper away from you, push across the work (Fig. 97): the slight bow in the tool will reduce the chance of the edges digging into the veneer surface. Remove any small shavings from the thicker, protruding veneers, so there is no fear of contaminating the light veneers with the shavings of the darker veneers.

An uneven surface may be flattened relatively quickly using the scraper, but do practise first, and if possible ask an experienced cabinet maker to demonstrate the technique before attempting to use it on your masterpiece.

This is only an interim process, and not an essential one, and you must still carry out sanding.

Don't forget that the object of the exercise is to produce not only a smooth surface but more importantly a flat one. It is essential therefore when sanding a surface to work from a flat plane which is relatively hard. Speeding the process up by using a power orbital sander is not the answer. The backing material to the sanding sheet is a soft rubber and will follow the contours of the original surface, simply rounding off the edges of the harder veneers and abrading away the softer veneers and making the

problem worse. Edges of the work will also take more pressure and a real danger exists of rubbing through the veneer to the backing board underneath.

We find that the best method is to use a large cork-faced sanding block with a single layer of 150 grade silicon carbide paper wrapped round it and to work over the surface in the direction of the most prominent grain flow – usually this is parallel with an edge. It is important to keep at least three-quarters of the sanding block's face over the surface being rubbed down (Fig. 92) as any greater overhang will result in the edges and corners being rubbed through. If carried out correctly there is very little danger of rubbing through the veneers.

At this stage the sense of touch is a much better guide than the eyes to the flatness of the work. When you judge the surface to be flat you can improve its quality by using a finer grade of silicon carbide paper, say 240 grade. This should be sufficiently fine; any tiny scratches will disappear under the polish.

Edges and backs of flat subjects must also be prepared to the same degree of flatness, but this is usually a lot quicker and easier due to the fact that single sheets of relatively soft veneers (e.g. sapele) are usually used for this purpose. Thin edges can be

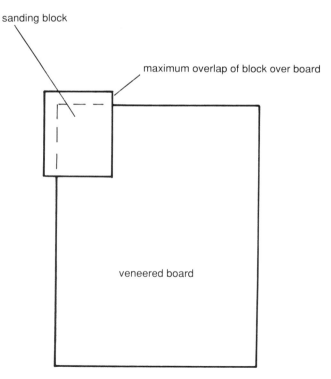

Fig. 92 Maximum overlap of the sanding block when rubbing down the veneered board, block, box etc.

a problem as it is difficult to keep these narrow strips square and flat. Fixing the work vertically in a woodworking vice or workmate and holding the sanding block in two hands can improve the quality of the edges enormously.

Boxes, clocks, etc., must all be prepared in the same way. Care must be taken with mouldings as these require sanding but you don't want to spoil the clean sharp edges. There are various ways of forming the abrasive paper into the form of the moulding but the use of a female forming block to wrap the paper round results in internal corners being missed and external corners being rounded off.

The surface must now be cleaned. Usually a soft-bristled brush will work the wood dust out of the grain so it can be blown off the surface. Don't breathe in this dust; should you be at all allergic to dust then use a vacuum cleaner. You might even wish to wear a filter mask: some wood dust can be a particular irritant. Solvents (e.g. white spirit) are advocated by some marquetarians to clean the surface of the work, but we find this unnecessary with the methods and materials we use. Whatever you do, be thorough: once the polish has been applied, any dust particles in the grain will remain entombed for ever.

Now for the application of the polish, the application of the first coat being one of the best moments in any woodworking, but especially marquetry. All the various grains, textures and colours are now, at one stroke, transformed into brilliant highlights and contrasts as the various qualities of the grains come to life. In some cases it shows up where we were not as subtle in our veneer selection as we had intended and high contrasts appear where we planned a minor shade change. To reduce this problem it may be helpful to accumulate a veneer collection with half the sheet having an application of polish.

POLISHING

The main object of the polishing process is to enhance the beauty of the wood. We also wish to protect the wood from the effects of ultra violet light which, in time, will bleach out the colours of the brighter woods and deepen the colours of the very pale veneers with the result that contrast is lost and impact reduced. The surface must also be smooth to eliminate staining due to dust or liquids which may be splashed or spilt on to the surface. The polish

must therefore at least seal and preferably fill the voids in the grain to bring the surface to a flat finish.

An important consideration in the selection of a polish is its lack of staining property. Many varnishes and polishes are not perfectly clear and will produce an overall tone change which on a plain medium to dark veneered piece of furniture will go unnoticed. However, when almost white veneers are incorporated in a picture or parquetry design the change shows up as a yellowing of the veneer and a reduction in the overall contrast.

CELLULOSE SANDING SEALER

This is one of the cheapest and most popular materials for finishing flat surfaces such as pictures and is one of the best in terms of transparency as well as being a hard finish with which a high gloss can be produced. It is best applied not by paintbrush but by rubbing it into the surface with the ball of the finger: use the finger cut from a rubber glove as protection.

As the filler and the cellulose elements of this sealer separate in a relatively short time they must be mixed thoroughly before you begin. Then put a small amount in the lid of a jar (not plastic or the cellulose will melt it) and start work. Rub the sealer gently into the surface of the veneer with a circular motion, working across the surface in lines covering about 5×5 cm (2×2 in.) at a time; the first coat will dry in a few seconds.

Apply the second and subsequent coats in the same way, continuing the circular rubbing action until you detect a slight drag as the previous coat softens and the two coats jell together. As the surface builds up the setting time increases but it is rarely more than 10 minutes.

The sequence of application of sealer to a picture is to coat the face and sides, then the back and sides. When this has been repeated three times the faces will have three coats and the sides six coats. The extra coats to the sides will compensate the fact that their small area rubs down a lot easier than the faces.

About an hour after the third coat is applied the surfaces can be rubbed down lightly to remove the high spots and give about 90 per cent flatness. This is determined by holding the surface up at an acute angle to the light and looking across the surface: the flattened surface will appear dull and untouched while low areas will still be bright. Fig. 93 attempts to show this inspection process, and the illustration shows a surface about 95 per cent flat.

A 250 grade silicon carbide paper is about the

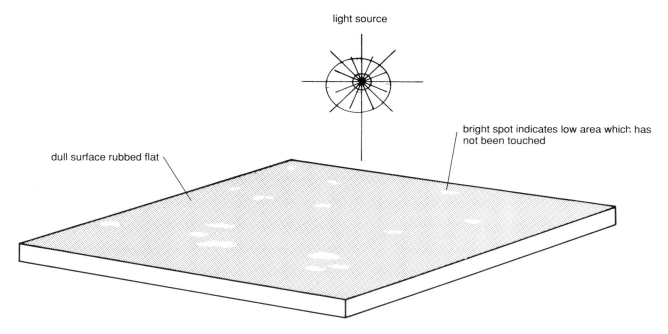

Fig. 93   Checking for flatness

right grade for this stage. It is more than possible that you will rub through the surface polish at this point, but that is to be expected as the object of the first few coats is to fill the pores in the grain only and not to try to achieve a polished surface.

Apply a further three coats down to a 95 per cent flatness and follow up with another three coats which you should aim to rub down to a 98 per cent flatness.

Note: Problems may now have become apparent if this is the first time you have attempted this process, the most frustrating of which is to keep rubbing through the polish to expose the veneer surface. This can occur as a result of one of several faults. Your rubbing-down technique may be too vigorous or you may be going too far over the edge of the board with the sanding block, which results in the edges only being rubbed through. Another, more likely, alternative is that the original surface was not flat. Try a straight edge across the surface to see if any defects in flatness are visible and if so you should continue to sand the surface with 150 grade silicon carbide paper until it is flat, and then start the process of polishing all over again, having learnt a valuable lesson in finishing. A surface which is not flat will never produce a good surface finish and layers of polish will never compensate for an uneven surface.

When you have reached a 98 per cent flat surface,

with however many coats of polish it takes, reduce the grit size of the abrasive paper. At this stage a wet-and-dry waterproof paper is preferable. This is used by touching the surface of the paper into a shallow tray of water to which a little washing-up liquid has been added. Wet-and-dry paper of 300 and 600 grade are used to achieve the 100 per cent flat surface required for a perfect finish.

But the surface is still dull. To achieve a gloss change to an abrasive slurry applied with a soft cloth. A car colour restorer is excellent but metal polishes and burnishing creams have a similar effect. A true high gloss is obtained only after a great deal of elbow grease has been applied and the final result depends on the amount of time you are prepared to devote to this activity. Don't attempt a gloss finish on anything other than a perfect surface as the small blemishes will show up badly, whereas a matt finish will hide these small defects.

Some subjects need, and some marquetarians always prefer, a matt or semi-matt finish. This does not come about as a result of the sealer used, but by the finishing process used. Having reached the 600 grade abrasive paper stage continue with a wire wool of 0000 or 40 grade. Rub this over the surface with the same action as used to apply the polish; it will soon give the surface a sheen. A slightly higher grade of finish (high sheen/low gloss) can be obtained by applying beeswax polish with the wire wool.

ACID-CATALYSED LACQUER

This material is a clear two-part plastic giving a very tough finish. Once mixed up a reaction starts – the warmer the room the shorter the reaction time. Storage in a refrigerator in a well-sealed jar will slow down the cure time of the mixed lacquer and catalyst and it may then last a few weeks. It is also best to store the fine-haired paintbrush in the jar as cleaning is rarely 100 per cent effective. A special thinner is available, but this is used for thinning down the first coat rather than cleaning paintbrushes.

The mixed lacquer can be used on wood which has been sealed with cellulose sealer and rubbed flat, or direct on to the veneer with a little thinner added to the first coat. Apply it with a brush to give a very generous covering and as soon as it is touch dry (about 10–25 minutes) apply a second coat, brushing at right angles to the first coat. Repeat this process about six to eight times then leave the surface for at least 24 hours before rubbing down and finish polishing in the same way as with the cellulose sealer.

Two words of warning

First, the process requires that the coats gel together. Should you wait for longer than an hour between coats you may find that on rubbing down a Newton ring effect occurs as you rub through the various layers of lacquer. Similarly, rubbing down is much easier if carried out within a few days of applying the lacquer, after which it will become fully hard. Second, the fumes from the curing lacquer are unpleasant and if you work in the house close the door to the room to reduce the effect on other occupants and open the window to ventilate the room!

ACRYLIC VARNISH

This is a relatively new development in the field of finishing products and may well be improved further over the next few years. The object is to reduce the number of solvent-based products on the market which are environmentally unfriendly.

It is claimed that it is non-flammable, non-toxic, it will not yellow and that it has a very low odour level (a definite advantage over acid-catalysed lacquer). Being water based it has one disadvantage: it is wise not to use it on veneers that have been stuck down with a water-based PVA adhesive as it may soften the glue and allow the veneer to rise. The solution is to use a non-water based adhesive (contact adhesive, thermo-setting adhesive or Cascamite) or apply

sanding sealer as a sealing coat before applying the acrylic varnish.

A brush is used to apply the varnish, but this should have synthetic bristles which pick up the varnish better and give a finer finish. Wet-and-dry paper should be used to rub down between coats which can be applied every two hours. The final coat can be burnished with a car paint colour restorer.

FRENCH POLISH

Woodworkers may well be tempted to use this traditional process. The most transparent of the French polishes, made from bleached de-waxed shellac, would be suitable for large areas, but would be frustrating to apply to small areas, and even this polish will give a slight darkening and hence a slight loss of contrast on marquetry.

SHELLAC SANDING SEALER

This is used in a similar way to French polish with similar results. We use it for items such as chess boards when we make several for sale at craft fairs.

OIL AND WAX

These do not give a practical finish on marquetry. The initial effect is of no more than a slight loss of contrast but they will soon gather dust and subsequent polishing will result in further contrast loss. They also give little protection against ultra violet light which in time will bleach out the colour in the veneers.

HANGING

Marquetry pictures, as opposed to decoration on pieces of woodwork, usually require hanging in some way. A number of commercial screw-on systems are available as well as many home-made devices similar to the mirror plate method. We use a very simple, cheap and effective method which has never yet been known to fail.

What you will need

- A hand drill. You may use an electric drill when you are more confident, but take care!
- A short length of dowel about 6 mm (^{1}/4 in.) diameter. A dark wood is better, but Ramin is

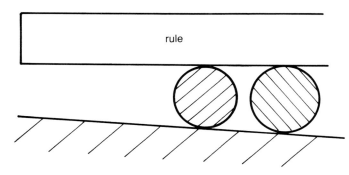

Fig. 94 Checking diameter similarity

suitable and is far more readily available. This is cut to lengths of 6 to 9 mm ($^{1}/_{4}$ to $^{3}/_{8}$ in.) depending on the thickness of the mounting board.

- A drill of the same diameter as the dowel, see Fig. 94 for a means of checking the size.
- A length of strong cord. Woven nylon is a suitably strong material.

The process of attaching the cord must be carried out after the back is sealed and polished. It is as well to leave it until the front and edges are also finished, but because the back will finish with no protrusions it is possible to polish, or if necessary repolish, the front face, after the cord is attached.

Method

1. Mark the back of the board where the cord is to be attached. Don't forget to place your picture on a soft surface (an old piece of carpet is ideal) to prevent the face being scratched. Fig. 95 gives the approximate positions of the fixing points if you are in doubt.

2. Now drill holes into the back, at the marked positions, to the required depth, which is usually about 3 mm ($^{1}/_{8}$ in.) less than the thickness of the board. This is where you can ruin your picture, but with a little care and forthought you shouldn't. A piece of tape, or other means of setting the depth of the hole on the drill, should prevent accidents Fig. 96). The hole must be at least 9 mm ($^{3}/_{8}$ in.) deep, and this can increase with boards over 12 mm ($^{1}/_{2}$ in.) thick.

3. Tie a knot in the end of the cord and trim it close to the knot. A spot of glue will prevent the knot coming untied. Cut a dowel 3 mm ($^{1}/_{8}$ in.) shorter than the depth of the hole. You can do this by pushing the dowel into the hole, marking to gauge the full depth, and subtracting the 3 mm ($^{1}/_{8}$ in.), which in turn also checks that the dowel fits the hole snugly. Cut a groove down the side of the dowel to accommodate the cord diameter Fig. 97.

4. Place the knot in the bottom of the hole with a drop of PVA adhesive, and push the dowel in so that the end is flush with the surface of the board, with

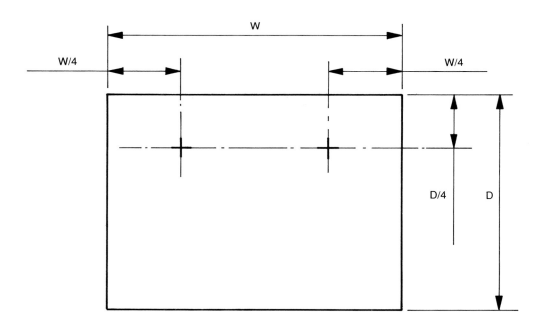

Fig. 95 Marking out the holes for hanging cards

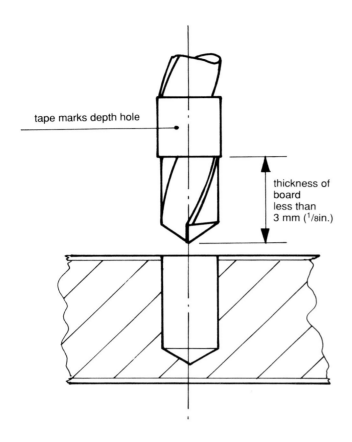

tape marks depth hole

thickness of
board
less than
3 mm ($\frac{1}{8}$in.)

Fig. 96 Safe drilling of holes in mounting board

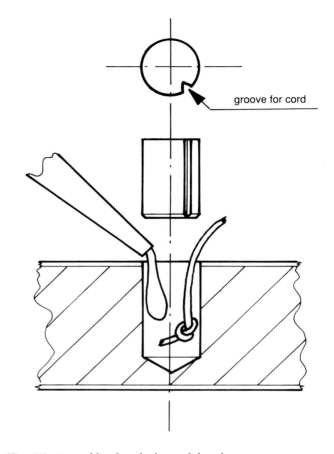

groove for cord

Fig. 97 Assembly of cord, glue and dowel

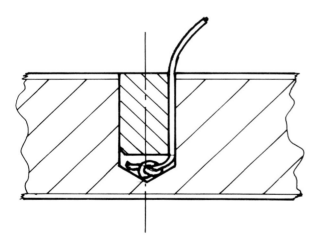

Fig. 98 Completed cord anchor

the cord coming up through the groove in the dowel. The finished assembly is shown in Fig. 98.

Repeat the process in the second hole, adjusting the knot in the cord to give the required length of loop for hanging.

The result is a flush back with only the cord protruding and a very strong anchor for the cord.

8

Step by Step Through Your First Picture

STEP BY STEP THROUGH YOUR FIRST PICTURE

The picture we have chosen to follow step by step is taken from an old greetings card and is shown as a line drawing in Fig. 99. The final result can be seen in the second colour section; we will call it 'The Old Mexican Church'. It has no trees as such, although some were added later, but it has good perspective and a range of colours we can match against the normal range of veneers we keep in our veneer box. We decided against giving a 'veneer key' so you can interpret the picture to suit your own taste and what veneers you have available. We used the following: maple, magnolia, sycamore, dark walnut, magnolia burr and harewood (various).

THE INITIAL TRACING

Start by tracing the picture. You can adapt the design to make it more suitable for marquetry in general, and for your own standard of skill in particular. For example, you could break up the left-hand wall with a tall shrub or sparsely foliaged tree, add more windows, or move the tree stumps to the right to allow a fence or low wall to be added along the near side of the road.

To simplify matters we will copy the card as it stands.

Try to avoid using a rule at this stage. Few buildings of this type have absolutely straight edges and to impose perfect lines will kill the interest.

PICTURE SIZE

The original card is approximately 100 × 140 mm high (4 × 5¹/₂ in.) and therefore we will increase its

size to twice the linear dimensions (four times the area). The traditional way of doing this is to divide the original tracing into squares, say 10 mm (¹/₂ in.) square, and repeat the same pattern and number of squares on a larger sheet enlarged to the scale required, 20 mm (1 in.) squares giving a suitable enlargement for this subject. The picture is then redrawn to the larger scale using the new grid as a guide to retain relative size and position as well as the original perspective.

You can also use a pantograph: if you do not have access to one, see Fig. 100 to construct one.

The modern, and easy, method is to have your tracing enlarged on a photocopier. Our picture was enlarged by the latter method to two and a half times the size of the original postcard as shown in Fig. 101.

FINAL DRAWING

You can now either use the enlarged copy or take a tracing from the enlargement. Tracing paper can sometimes be an advantage as you can see the picture take shape through it and hence against the complete design. In this case we used the copy direct.

SELECTING THE WASTER

First find a suitable sky-effect veneer or waster on to which we transfer the design using carbon paper. If possible this should be a smooth, easily cut veneer. If available a freak veneer may sometimes be used, such as a stained obeche, or one with especially effective grain markings like American gum, which was used at a slight angle to give the picture added depth. Orangewood can also be used to simulate a sunset. The ebony sky however, is not advised for the beginner as it is not easy to work. All these sky veneers are shown in the second colour section. While dealing with the sky it is worth stating that we would hardly ever cut in clouds, as these will always look like cottom wool blobs.

If the chosen picture has a low horizon, say 70 per cent sky, it would be worth picking a freak veneer for this. Conversely, if the sky is only one-third of the picture with the foregound rising up quite high in the form of buildings, trees, etc., a freak veneer would be wasted and the skyline become too cluttered; in this case a fairly plain veneer such as avodire with just a slight slanted mottle might be the best choice.

Fig. 99 Line drawing used as plan for Old Mexican Church

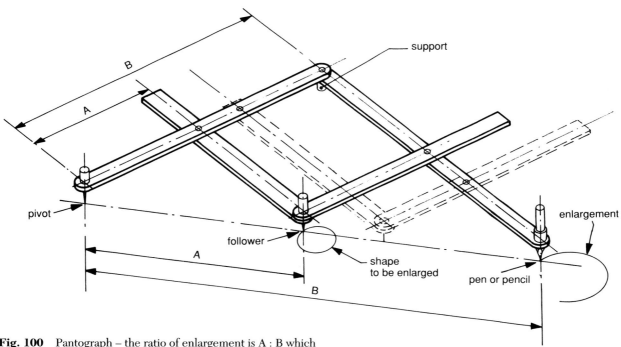

Fig. 100 Pantograph – the ratio of enlargement is A : B which can be changed by adjusting the pivot points as shown. Note that pivot, follower & pencil must be in line

Fig. 101 A range of enlargements

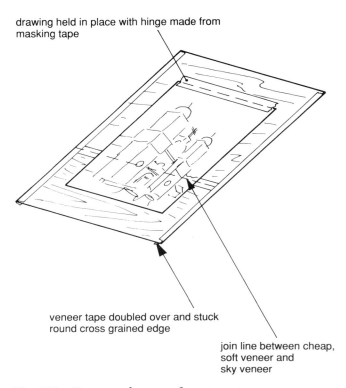

drawing held in place with hinge made from masking tape

veneer tape doubled over and stuck round cross grained edge

join line between cheap, soft veneer and sky veneer

Fig. 102 Picture ready to transfer onto waster

PREPARING THE WASTER

To save wasting the more exotic woods add a piece of cheap sap walnut, which is an easy veneer to cut, below the horizon line (Fig. 102). Make the joint with veneer tape as this area will be removed during the cutting of the picture, hence the term waster.

PROTECTING THE WASTER

The waster, when prepared, should be about 30 mm (over 1 in) larger than the proposed finished size. Gummed tape is then stuck down both cross-grain edges, half the tape width over the edge so that it can be folded over on to the face side and secured by rubbing down well. This is to protect these edges from splitting as, during the cutting and gluing processes, the waster will be turned and manhandled a great deal (also shown in Fig. 102).

TRANSFERRING THE DESIGN TO THE WASTER

When all the preparation is complete place your tracing in position on the waster and select your preferred position (another good reason for using tracing paper) before taping down the top edge with

masking tape to form a hinge which will remain in place until the picture is finished (see again Fig. 102). You will be working from the back of the final mounted picture, which will be the reverse of what you see on the working side. If the subject is a recognizable view or subject, or for some aesthetic reason you wish it to be the same hand as the original design, you must turn over the tracing and show the opposite hand (a further excellent reason for using tracing paper). As it is so much easier to follow an original design of the same hand, our picture will be worked on that way and hence reversed when mounted!

Now place carbon paper, black not blue, under the tracing paper and draw the entire picture over so it is carboned on to the background waster. This may seem a waste of time in some respects, as much of the transferred drawing will be lost when the surrounding areas are cut away and will require transferring again on to the new veneer, but it may help in initial selection of veneers if you have a complete picture in front of you before you begin cutting.

CUTTING THE PICTURE

Start by cutting some of the larger pieces and set them in place first to build up the structure of the picture quickly: worry about the smaller detail later. And don't use a straight edge; it gives entirely the wrong effect. For these large pieces use veneer tape stuck on the face side to hold them in place, and then PVA adhesive, as PVA alone is not enough to secure them.

If you are right-handed, begin towards the top left-hand corner and work down and across to avoid continually working over your completed work. Top right-hand corner for left-handers! In this picture we started on the shaded walls on the left-hand side. Maple was used to form the two facing turret walls with a very light harewood for the walls in shadow. It is important to remember which direction the sun is coming from, to get shadows and shaded areas all corresponding.

Varying shades of sycamore and maple were used throughout the picture, these also being used on alternate sides to achieve natural and more subtle difference in colour (Figs. 103 and 104).

Having cut and added all the large pieces, hinge the drawing back to cover the part-complete picture and again transfer the smaller detail, which was cut away, to the veneer as shown in Fig. 105.

Fig. 103   The picture hinged to the top of waster with the design transferred to the waster and the first few pieces cut in. This is the cutting side, the side which will be glued down

Fig. 104   Further progress, viewed from the face side

Commencing the cutting in this way not only encourages you by building the picture quickly but will help increase cutting experience for tackling the small more intricate pieces to come. When you have gained some experience and are attempting more complex designs it is often better to start with the background, cutting the foreground features into this. It is possible thus to avoid interfering with the outline of the main objects which can become nicked if the background is cut up to them.

HINTS ON CUTTING

As with the drawing, you should never use a straight edge to cut against in pictorial marquetry.

When creating shadows try to avoid a black-white chessboard effect by looking for subtle changes of just a few shades difference.

Fig. 105   At the same stage of working as Fig. 104, but viewed from the working side

The curved pieces of architecture over the towers may cause some problems in cutting due to the veneer breaking across the short grain. This can be avoided by first applying veneer tape to the back of the veneer, and in severe cases to both sides of the veneer.

THE HEDGES

The last pieces to be added are the hedges which means that the complex shapes have to be cut only once into the walls that cover this area. For the hedges we used magnolia burr which has a greenish tinge. Because of the complex shape, cover both the face side of the burr and the picture (the underside as you work), in veneer tape. Although these hedges tend to look a little like lost jigsaw pieces there is not much option unless you use fragmentation.

For this complex piece of cutting use the sandwich method. Fix the burr with masking tape to the face side of the picture, over the area of the bushes. Working on the back of the picture, as normal, stab cut round the outline; this enables you to keep to the tight curves without losing the point of your knife blade. Push the point of the blade down deep enough to ensure an impression on the burr beneath.

Don't attempt to cut the full length of the hedge in one piece. Apart from being much more difficult it does not look as good, and on our picture we cut about one third of the length at a time. The veneer tape on the burr helped to keep it intact as burrs can sometimes be quite fragile when cut into intricate shapes.

Having cut in the magnolia some smaller pieces of walnut burr were cut in in an attempt to add some depth.

FINAL TOUCHES

Because the near wall looked a bit bare we decided to add a small tree to add interest in this corner. This was done using the same method as we used for the hedges.

When your picture is complete it is a good idea to place it on display rather than rushing headlong into the mounting operation, to be sure that you are entirely satisfied with it. Support the veneer on a piece of plywood and prop it up in a prominent place so that you can study it when passing or when relaxing – but not in direct sunlight, or over the fire or radiator! You can then make any additions or alterations before you lay the picture, when it will become almost impossible.

FRAMING AND MOUNTING

FRAMING

Cut the picture to size as described in Chapter 7, making sure that all of the waster part of the picture is cut away.

As this is a typical early picture we decided on a relatively simple white-black-white stringer and a border of sapele. A fancy stringer could have been incorporated, but the picture would have to have been cut down to match up the pattern at the corners. Chapter 7 covers the process of mitre cutting.

MOUNTING BOARD

To mount, cut the piece of MDF 3 mm (^{1}/8 in.) smaller than the picture size, checking that the board and its edges are square. We used 16 mm (^{5}/8 in.) board, but 12 mm (^{1}/2 in.) thick board would also be suitable for this size of picture.

LAYING

Follow the correct order of laying (i.e. back, top and bottom edges, side edges, face). If you have a press available, use this to lay the back and face veneers, using PVA adhesive, and use gluefilm for the edges. If not, choose a contact adhesive as directed in Chapter 7.

PREPARING THE SURFACES

Whether you use PVA in a press or contact adhesive it is as well to leave the picture to settle overnight before commencing the sanding and finishing operation. First clean the gummed tape from the face by gently scraping with an old knife, chisel or heel of the cutting blade. Don't use a scraper for this task as it will tear any cross grain and damage the veneer. Far better to start with a medium grade silicon carbide paper (120 grade) and finish off with 240 grade, sanding the edges first, then the back and finally the front face.

Clean off all traces of dust and dirt with a stiff brush.

APPLYING THE POLISH

In this case we chose sanding sealer. Apply with the ball of the middle finger which holds just enough sealer to cover an area of about 40×40 mm (1 $^1/_2$ in. square). Apply the coats front–sides, back–sides until back and front have had three coats and the edges six. Chapter 7 describes how to obtain various finishes. Here we opted for a gloss finish although it can fairly be claimed that the reflection off this surface can make it difficult to view.

PART

2

9

Projects

In Part 2 we try to bring together most of the techniques described in Part 1 in a series of applied projects and pictures.

Almost any piece of woodwork can be enhanced by the application of well selected and prepared veneers. It can also reduce the cost of woodwork projects by making it possible to use cheaper softwood or inexpensive and more staple man-made boards (such as MDF) rather than large pieces of solid hardwood. We can also claim that the very small amount of wood used to cover large areas with veneer is far more environmentally friendly.

In many cases the applied work is simply the application of pictorial marquetry to suitable surfaces on any wood construction, and those pieces with reasonably large flat surfaces are the most suitable.

When considering a project involving marquetry our first thought must be to consider the area available for our inlay work. Board games will need to be covered completely and are ideal objects for this work. Smaller items such as letter racks, magazine racks, bowls and clocks offer much less scope, and a greater amount of planning and thought must be given at the design stage to make the best use of the available area.

This part of the book is divided into several sections, each of which contains a selection of interesting and challenging projects.

PICTURE GALLERY

These pictures (shown opposite and overleaf) have been selected to illustrate different styles of pictorial marquetry and to show how the various techniques described in previous chapters can be applied.

'THIRD AND GOAL'

A detailed picture created from three veneers which have areas of variable shades in the grain pattern. Most parts of the players were cut from walnut and the background waster is sycamore, to give maximum projection to the players. No border has been used but a double-edge banding in walnut creates a thin dark line round the picture.

'HARD TIMES'

A picture that needed no fancy sky or foreground, but was faded off into the background of horse chestnut by the use of light grey harewoods.

The face of Folly Gradgrind (the old gentleman) was cut into a small piece of waste veneer and transferred to the full-size design by the reverse window method. All shadows were created by using light and dark pieces of the same veneer, or single pieces cut from the heartwood/sapwood interface. The letters on the poster had to be in reverse when working from the back – no problem if tracing paper is used to transfer a design.

The picture was finished without a border, but fine ebony stringers create a geometrical pattern in the corners.

TALL SHIP

An example of harewood used to effect in a sky; when this piece of veneer was obtained this type of picture immediately came to mind. The sea, rather than being made up of one sheet, became a patchwork of small pieces of sycamore, walnut and various harewoods. The sea and sky complement each other. The appearance of curvature in the sails was obtained by sand shading.

The picture has been framed in a single piece of sapele with the addition of fancy ribbon-work.

'TOY SHOP'

Instead of the usual rather flat-looking border, this frame was turned on a lathe, but could quite easily be made using a router.

Reflections from window glass are always difficult to reproduce in wood: study photographs of similar subjects before attempting something like this. Snow scenes too have their problems: the marquetry joints between light veneers often show up as thin dark lines, even when they are tightly cut. Avoid this type of picture unless the light areas can be constructed from single sheets of veneer.

This picture was adapted from a Victorian-style Christmas card.

Third and Goal – a three veneer picture (Alan Townsend)

Hard Times – a typical marquetry picture (David Middleton)

Tall Ship – note the unusual mount (Alan Townsend)

Toy Shop – a circular picture in a round frame (Alan Townsend)

Chaplin Clock – an example of the Inverted U Clock (Ted Higgs)

The Old Mexican Church – these four pictures show the effect of using alternative veneers for the waster:

American gum is particularly effective for the sky with its grain markings

Orangewood is ideal for creating a sunset

Ebony is quite striking, but it is not advised for th beginner as it is not easy to work

Avodire makes a similarly interesting sky

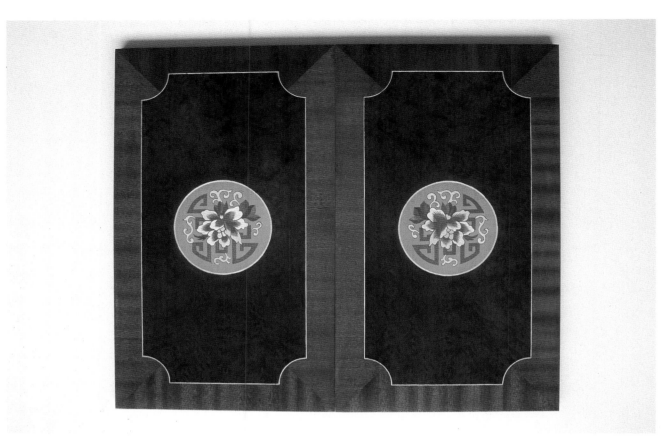

Doors for a TV cabinet – (Alan Townsend)

Table top – a Chinese design adapted for marquetry
(David Middleton)

Sweet jar – marquetry applied to a tunnel cylinder
(Alan Townsend)

Games boards – a selection of parquetry base games boards

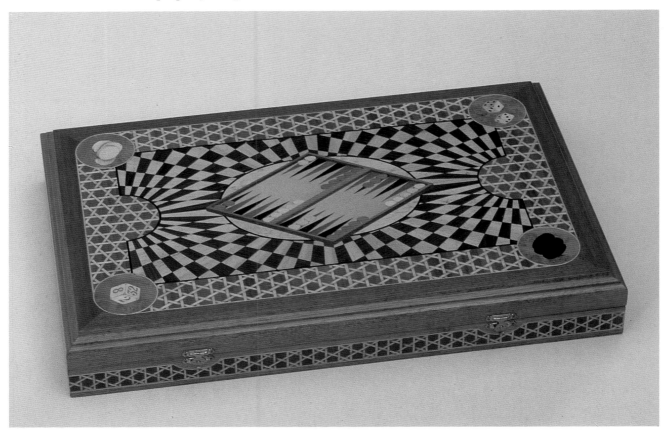

Backgammon box – parquetry applied to the top of a games box
(David Middleton)

Jewellery and 'knick-knack' boxes, and to a lesser extent cigarette boxes, have always made very acceptable presents, as well as profitable items for sale at craft fairs. It is not easy to obtain suitable blank (unveneered) boxes and although a range of small sycamore and lime boxes are sold for pyrography (pokerwork) many of these have rounded edges making it difficult to apply veneer. Some boxes are available with thin plywood top and bottom about 3 mm (1/8 in.) thick which are easily veneered, or you may prefer to make a box yourself.

We will concentrate on those we can make without the use of elaborate dovetail joints as these would be a waste of good cabinet-making skills, and valuable time, if we are to eventually veneer all the sides and top.

CUBE CONSTRUCTION BOX

Let us start with the cube construction. This method will require four sides just butted together and glued as shown in Fig. 106, and requires the minimum amount of skill or tools. In most cases it is easier to make up the panels for the box and construct the box to the required dimensions afterwards.

Method of box construction
1. Cut the short sides to length.
2. Cut the long sides to the length of the box less the thickness of the two ends. If possible the sides should be made of hardwood.
3. Glue together and clamp.
4. Cut the top and bottom from 6 mm (1/4 in.) plywood and glue both in place to form an enclosed box or 'cube'. Level as necessary.
5. Apply the prepared veneers using a contact adhesive, first the ends, then front and back, finally top and bottom.
6. Sand all faces flat, apply sealer and rub down to a flat finish.

7. Saw through the side pieces to form the lid to give the section shown in Fig. 107.
8. Sand flat the cut surfaces.
9. Fit hinges, line inside (if required) and polish the outside.

Notes:
A number of techniques and variations can be employed with this basic method which include:

- PVA adhesive or Cascamite may be preferred for the application of the veneer, but this requires a slight change in the construction to prevent distortion during clamping, which could result in blisters in the surface. To prevent this, cut strips of waste wood, the same depth as the sides, to fit across the width of the box. Place these in position as shown in Fig. 110 (don't glue them), before the top and bottom are glued in place. These strips will support the long sides and top and bottom during clamping and can easily be removed when the lid is cut. The short side should not need support.
- If you decide to prepare the marquetry panels after the box is made remember to allow for the thickness of the veneer at the edges.
- If the design of the panels requires a continuation of the pattern on the side panel between the base and the lid (as in the ivy box, Fig. 111) then the thickness of the sawcut (the kerf) must be allowed for. To do this cut the completed side panel veneers at the proposed lid line, insert a strip of waste veneer of approximately 1.5 mm (1/16 in.) width, or ideally a white stringer, and tape it in place. When applied to the box this becomes the cutting line.
- To prevent damage to the veneers when cutting the lid scribe two lines with a marking gauge either side of the saw cut. With the packing pieces inside the box it is also possible to hold the box, top to bottom, in a vice to make sawing the lid easier and give greater security while sawing.
- Sanding the cut faces of the lid and base with a sanding block usually results in an ill-fitting lid. A better method is to secure a full sheet of 100 to

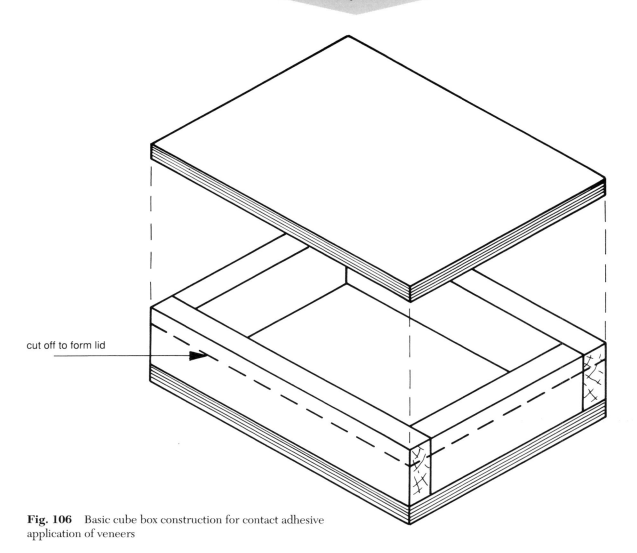

cut off to form lid

Fig. 106 Basic cube box construction for contact adhesive application of veneers

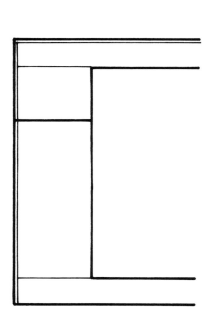

Fig. 107 Basic cube construction

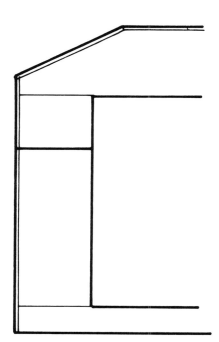

Fig. 108 A chamfer formed on the thicker lid section

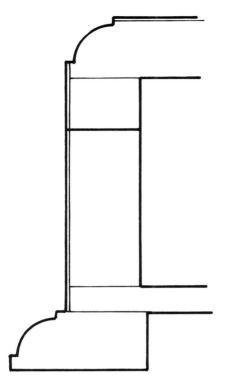

Fig. 109 Moulded lid and feet

Fig. 111 Chamfered lid of the 'ivy covered box' showing the pattern following over the chamfer

120 grade sandpaper to a flat board with cow gum or drawing pins and, using a rotary action, gently smooth away the cut surface on the lid and base.

• By using a solid wood top piece up to 25 mm (1 in.) thick it is possible to chamfer the lid with a large disc sander or plane as can be seen in the ivy box (see Figs. 108 and 111). Making the top in hardwood to match the background veneer also allows you to mould the edges with the router, after the veneer is applied (see Fig. 109).

• The rebates for the hinges, which are cut half in the lid and half in the base, can be removed with a straight cutter in the router or with the saw and chisel.

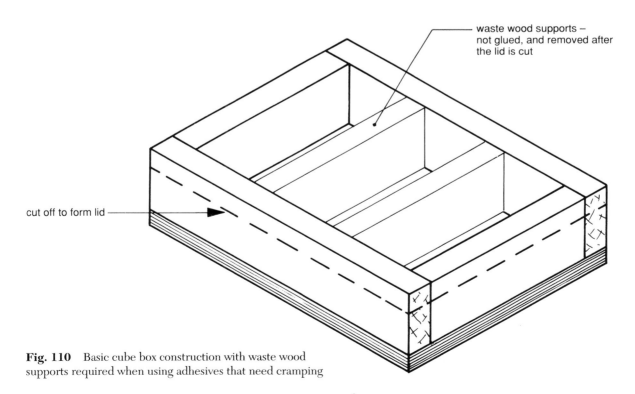

waste wood supports – not glued, and removed after the lid is cut

cut off to form lid

Fig. 110 Basic cube box construction with waste wood supports required when using adhesives that need cramping

Fig. 112 Casket jewellery box

CASKET JEWELLERY BOX (Fig. 112)

This box was made by the 'cube' method with the addition of a moulded base and inset half-round edge mouldings. The lid and lower part of the base were also shaped, using the disc sander. The

Fig. 113 Clamping strips used to hold the side veneers in place while the glue sets

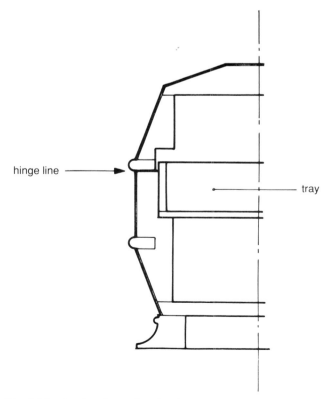

hinge line →

tray

Fig. 114 Section through casket box

Fig. 115 The prepared lid veneer as a development – in the process of being fitted

prepared veneers were applied with a PVA adhesive, using a shaped piece of timber to enable pressure to be applied using G-cramps. This can be seen in Fig. 113 together with the piece of polythene necessary to prevent the wood clamping bar becoming stuck to the box. Fig. 114 shows a section through the box.

The preparation of the lid veneer was carried out on a quartered burr with all the facets marked out and made as a single development (see Fig. 115). The veneers were then applied with a butt joint at the junction of the angles, as illustrated in Fig. 81.

MITRED BOX

This method makes good use of the sanding disc. It enables us to apply the veneers before assembling the box, which can be a great advantage.

Method
1. Cut the sides and ends to the correct finished length.
2. The panels of marquetry which have already been prepared can now be laid direct using PVA or a two-part adhesive and a press. By applying the veneer to flat uniform strips there should be no problem with support pieces being required. The inside and exposed top edge can also be veneered at this stage if required.

3. After the glue has cured you can cut the mitres on the corners. This can best and most accurately be achieved on the disc sander using the protractor guide (Fig. 116). Cut the mitre down so that the veneer is exposed at the sharp end of the mitre.

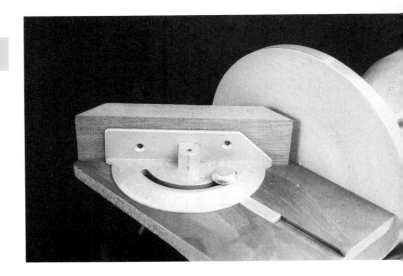

Fig. 116 Mitred corners being prepared on the disc sander

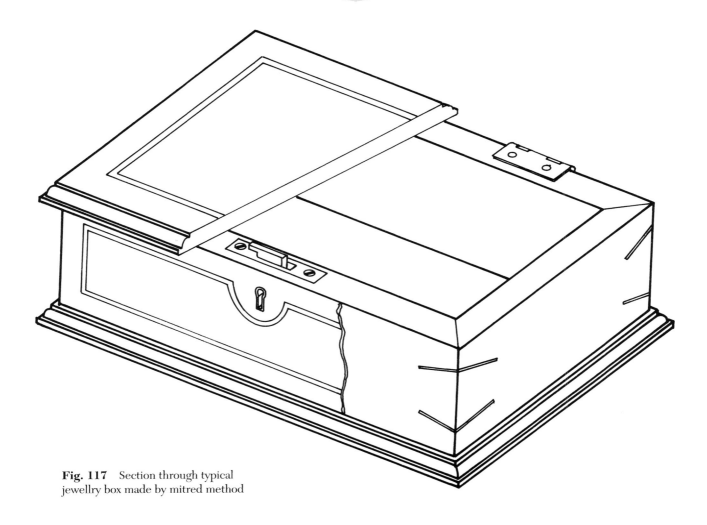

Fig. 117 Section through typical jewellry box made by mitred method

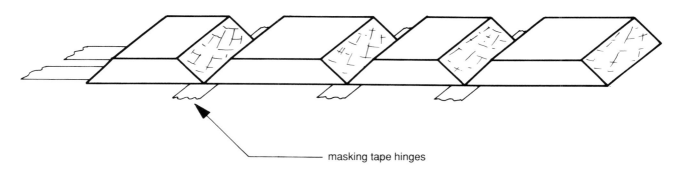

masking tape hinges

Fig. 118 Sides of mitred box taped together ready to form the frame

4. At this stage it is also essential to seal and polish the surfaces, a task which is relatively easy on the small rectangular pieces.

5. Now lay the four sides out in order and apply masking tape to join the sharp edges which will form the corners. Apply tape also at one end ready to form the joint when the sides are assembled into a box. The arrangement is shown in Figs. 117–18.

6. Apply some PVA adhesive to one face of each mitre joint and bring the mitres together using the masking tape as a hinge as shown in Fig. 119. The fourth joint is formed with the tape – you have

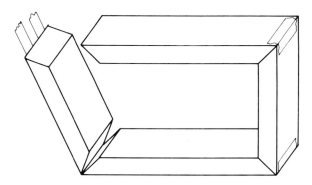

Fig. 119 Mitred box with side-end hinges in the process of being formed into the box frame

grain of the main face veneer must be 90° to the compensating veneer. This serves two purposes:

- To ensure that the timber remains flat. A veneer applied with its grain direction the same as that of the timber may twist and bow the lid.
- In time, depending on the glue used, the timber may start to split slightly under stress and this will result in tiny hair cracks in the veneer. This usually only happens when you use an adhesive such as Cascamite which sets very hard and brittle. The compensating veneer should stabilize the surface. You should also bear this in mind if you use plywood for this sort of job.

produced the four sides of the box (Fig. 119). After checking for squareness place the assembly on a flat surface with a weight on the top to ensure it dries level.

7. Now make the top and bottom; here again it is best to leave this until the sides are assembled to obtain accurate sizes. Make these a little larger than the box dimensions so that the edges can be moulded, and with the addition of small feet your box takes on a period feel. For both top and bottom solid timber is preferable, for instance mahogany, but MDF makes an acceptable substitute as it is capable of moulding well and taking a stain to match the veneer used.

If you use solid mahogany in fairly large pieces to make the lid and it is not part of the 'cube', it is necessary to take precautions. First apply a 'compensating' veneer on both top and bottom which must lay at 90° to the grain of the lid; the

SHAPED BOX

If you use the mitre-type construction and are prepared to veneer the sides after construction it is possible to shape the sides. The basic construction is similar to that already described:

1. As before, the sides and ends are cut to the correct finished length, but this time calculated from the inside dimensions. The thickness of the front and sides must be increased to accommodate the curves. As the back will remain straight it can be thinner and hence save wood and reduce the amount of cutting required. The assembly can be seen in Fig. 120. When trying this for the first time it would be prudent to draw the plan view of the box full size.

2. Cut the mitres on the sanding disc; tape, glue and assemble as before (see also Fig. 120).

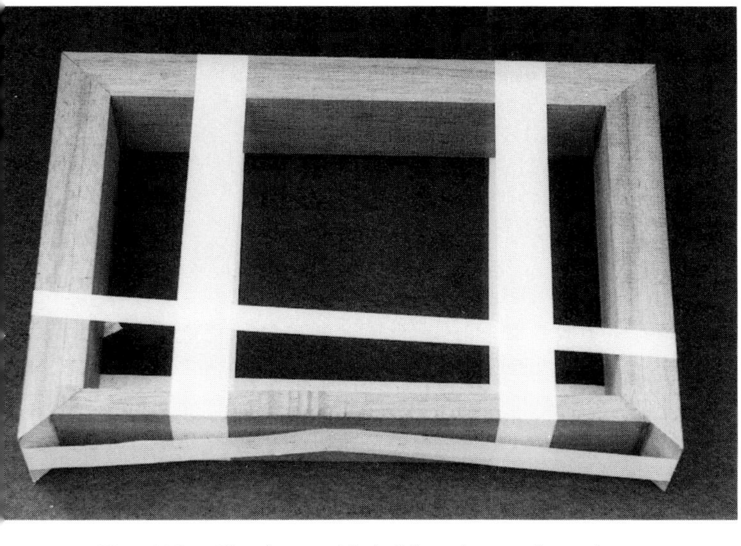

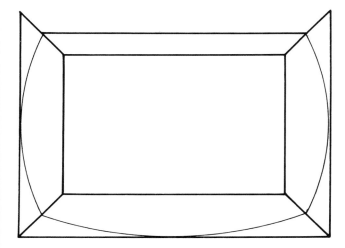

Fig. 120 Glued assembly held in place with masking tape

Fig. 121 Marked sides of curved sided box ready for cutting on the bandsaw – note the narrow rear section

Fig. 122 Bandsaw in use cutting the curved sides

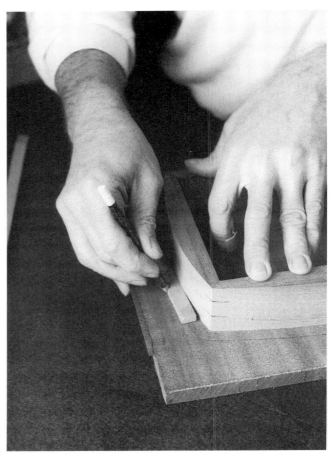

Fig. 124 Marking the base with the aid of a parallel wood strip of suitable width

Fig. 123 Strengthening the glued mitres with veneer

Fig. 125   Completed shaped box

3. Now mark out the bowed faces. Do this by tapping in a panel pin at each end of the side/front pieces. Push a plastic rule or thin piece of plywood against the pins until you have the required curve and mark with a pencil as shown in Fig. 121.

4. The curved sides can now be cut with a band saw (Fig. 122) and brought to a smooth finish on the sanding disc.

5. Make one or two cuts across each mitre using a thin-bladed saw (a junior hacksaw is ideal). Insert into these cuts pieces of glued veneer to give added strength to the mitres (these are known as 'veneer feathers'). The photograph (Fig. 123) shows the result at this stage. This process can be used on any mitred joint that will be covered with veneer.

6. Apply the prepared veneer to the curved surfaces as described in Chapter 7.

7. Draw out both the profiles for the base and lid using the space bar technique shown in Fig. 124.

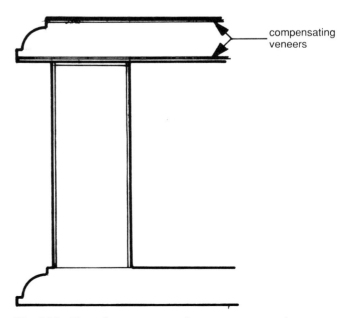

compensating veneers

Fig. 126   Typical cross-section of mitre construction box

Cutting with the band saw and smoothing on the disc sander are followed by veneer application and moulding as with the straight-sided mitred box.

The final section is shown in Fig. 126. This shows the veneered faces, and in particular the compensating veneers applied to the solid wood lid. Fig. 125 shows the completed box.

USE OF EXISTING BOXES

Cigar boxes can be used but they do tend to be rather flimsy. Old jewellery boxes are another possibility; if these are polished in any way the polish must be cleaned off back to the bare wood.

Another unlikely base for veneering is an empty drinking chocolate tin or similar. These can be veneered on the cylindrical surface using a contact adhesive, once the decorative covering has been cleaned off. Note that when the veneer is wrapped round the tin it is not finished with a straight joint; the joint follows the grain of the veneer to try to make it less visible. With a turned top and base, as added here, it is possible to produce quite a good-looking biscuit barrel, tea caddy (see second colour section) or whatever!

It is possible to produce the more basic designs very quickly in terms of time taken on the marquetry. The inverted 'U' shape clock (see Fig. 127) is about 225 by 125 mm (9 × 5 in.) in front elevation, but with the clock movement in place this only leaves us with an area of approximately 100 by 125 mm (4 × 5 in.) to cover with marquetry. The Napoleon's hat style (Fig. 128) gives even less area, and the complex design, in terms of woodwork, of the bracket clock (Fig. 129, p. 108) gives only a slightly greater area on each side.

INVERTED 'U' CLOCK (colour section)

The inverted 'U' shape can be made up of two or three thicknesses of either blockboard or MDF glued together sandwich fashion to form a block. On to the face side glue a 12 mm (1/2 in.) thick piece of hardwood – American walnut is excellent – to cover the entire surface. This is optional although it does allow you to rout out a small moulding round the

front edge which takes away some of the block's squareness. A solid block or a sandwich of solid pieces of timber is the ideal.

Now cut out the block as described in Chapter 7 (male–female method), and veneer up the sides and over the top using this technique.

A hole has to be cut through the block from front to back to accommodate the round bezel movement. You can do this with a hole saw or tank cutter which can be purchased to suit the exact size. This tool must be used on a pillar drill with the block clamped down. It may not cut through the thickness of the block, but can be cut from the back using the central drilled hole for location and to ensure accurate alignment.

For the demonstration clock we adapted a small bamboo design. The shape of the area left when the round clock-face is fitted allowed us to extend the bamboo design a little up both sides of the face.

When the marquetry is complete glue it to the face of the block then trim out the centre hole and prepare the surface for polishing. If staining is required on the side face or moulding you should now apply the polish to the areas not requiring stain

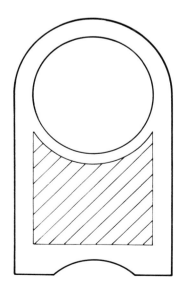

Fig. 127   Area available for marquetry on front of an inverted U-shaped clock

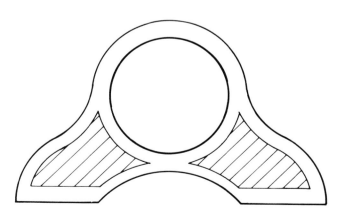

Fig. 128   Area available for marquetry on front of Napoleon's hat clock

Fig. 130 A rear view of the bracket clock showing the stages of build up of the base and top

Fig. 129 View of the marquetry on the side of the bracket clock

Fig. 131 The top moulding ready for assembly

as this will protect them from any splashes or runs. Finish the polishing at this stage, before any moulding is cut or added to the base, to avoid these areas of fine detail filling up with sealer so that they are very difficult to clean.

A fine ovalo moulding was routed round the front edge stopping about 35 mm (1 ½ in.) from the bottom on each side. Around the front and sides at the bottom we glued a thin moulding which was mitred on the corners, and out of the base we cut a shallow arc to lighten its appearance.

Apart from a very thin application of sanding sealer on the mouldings used to fill the grain and lightly rubbed down, it is best to give this type of work a cellulose spray finish. You don't get a finish of the same quality as you would for a large flat surfaces such as pictures, but it is quite satisfactory for these types of projects and will retain the crisp lines of the fine mouldings.

The Napoleon's hat clock can be made in exactly the same way using the same techniques.

BRACKET CLOCK

This clock is slightly more complex in terms of woodwork. On the other hand the marquetry panels on the sides use only the basic techniques to produce simple pictures.

The mouldings were all made using two or three different router cutters, mitred into the rectangular size of the clock, then built up one on top of the other, as shown in Figs. 132 and 133, to create a lavish-looking moulded top and bottom. The actual case is merely a box with a door and back which houses the movement. We have not given constructional details, but see the photographs Figs. 130 and 131.

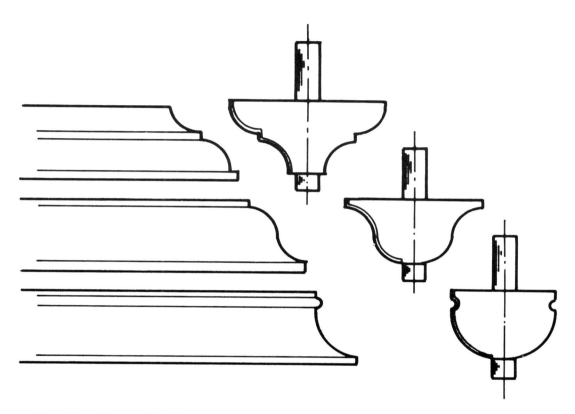

Fig. 132 Build-up of mouldings made with router cutters – top (hood) sections

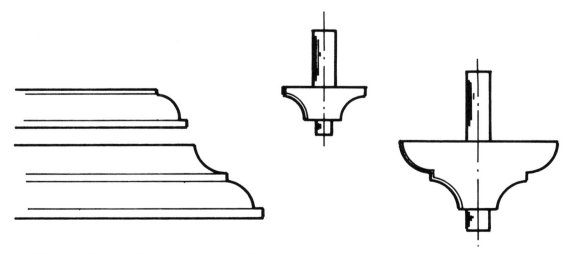

Fig. 133 Build-up mouldings made with router cutters for bracket clock – bottom sections

Fig. 134 Typical picture clock using the grain of the wood as a feature

Fig. 135 Inverted U Clock showing quartz mechanisms

PICTURE CLOCKS (Fig. 134)

This usually consists of a rectangular or square base board with the movement offset to one end or corner and a small picture or parquetry design in the space left, which can be quite large. If the open-hand style is used, with no bezel or face, the area available for marquetry is greatly increased. With this style of picture clock an overall landscape or view may be used with plastic numerals or digits fixed to the picture face, the movement being fixed to the back with the spindle for the hands projecting through a drilled hole. Consideration should be given at the design stage as to where the hole will be drilled for the movement; laying the hands on the picture face may help with the final positioning.

CLOCK MECHANISMS

A wide range of clock mechanisms is available of which the battery-driven quartz movements are particularly well suited to open-face picture clocks,

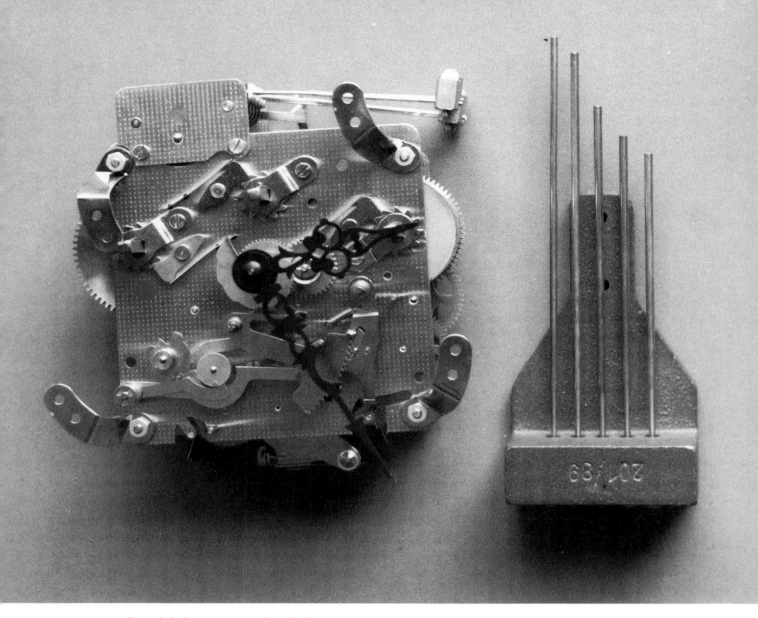

Fig. 136 A traditional clock movement with striker bars

especially when recessed in a turned clock frame. Traditional movements, as seen in Fig. 136 can be very expensive and need the very highest quality woodworking skills to justify their purchase.

Quartz movements with built-in bezels are attractive on small traditional clocks such as the ebony clock in Fig. 135. Weather instruments of matching styles are available and designs for weather stations can be fun to create using appropriate marquetry.

GAMES BOARDS

In terms of time, the most economical games board to produce is the chess board. A wide variety of light/dark veneer combinations is available and the surround of the board can be enhanced by incorporating parquetry designs. If required the squares can even be changed into more complex patterns requiring more traditional marquetry skills. Further woodworking skills may be called upon if a storage system for playing pieces is envisaged as part of the design. This may be in the form of a box with a removable or hinged lid, or a drawer system set under the playing surface.

A backgammon board is the next most obvious choice for a marquetry piece and could well be incorporated into a compendium of board games with storage. Cribbage boards also have good potential for parquetry design, requiring a very limited range of woodworking tools or skills. Finally, Chinese Checkers has the advantage, in terms of variety of work, of being played on a diamond, rather than a square-patterned board.

CHESS BOARD (colour section)

Two contrasting veneers are required for the alternating squares and it is advisable to choose those which are available in large flat sheets and are reasonably easy to cut. Aspen, maple, bird's eye maple (for a special effect), and sycamore are some suitable light veneers with mahogany, walnut and sapele being easy-to-cut darker shades. Ebony, purpleheart, rosewood and wenge are other attractive dark veneers but they can present problems in cutting.

Having selected the veneers you must ensure that the leaves are long enough; you need strips which are over nine times longer than their width. Cut the strips with a long-bladed knife to avoid the grain taking over the direction of cutting. After an initial straight edge has been cut maintain the width of the strips by using a straight edge of the correct width or by using the jig shown in Fig. 62 (p. 66). Five and four strips are required of the light/dark selection; it does not matter which has five.

It is normal to cut down the grain as this is the most economical method, but cutting at an angle is quite permissible and cutting one set on the cross grain can be very effective. For cutting across the grain it is better to return to a pointed blade as this will drag less, and it may be better to cut the long cross-grain strips from a straight-grained dark veneer (e.g. sapele) as it will be difficult to hide the joins in a light wood if you cannot get it in very wide sheets.

Now tape the strips together, shapes alternating, with veneer tape on the face side. It may also be as well to rub a little glue into the joints to add strength. Trim off the end of the assembled strips straight and square with the edge using a large try-square to set the straight edge true. From this end cut eight strips across the nine original strips which, when cut, now form lines of nine squares. It is as well to keep these in the order they are cut to reduce the chance of steps showing up if you have made any mistakes in the cutting.

With the strips lined up into their original layout, displace every other strip one square to the right (or left, or up, or down, depending on the way you lay them out) and tack in place with masking tape. Turning over, again tape the joints with veneer tape and trim off the odd square at each end (see Fig. 137).

The playing surface is now complete. The addition of stringers, particularly the fancy manufactured variety, and a border, applied as described in Chapter 7, should produce a finished article suitable to display the finest chess set.

CRIBBAGE BOARD (colour section)

The orthodox oblong cribbage board is small enough to present few problems when you lay the finished parquetry and will give you good initial practice before more demanding excursions into applied marquetry.

Fig. 137 The strips cut at 90° to produce squares, which are now offset to make the chess board pattern

The making techniques described are for small batch production of the boards. Individual designs can be produced by the window or various other methods.

First construct the two columns of six small oblongs, which are the blocks in which the peg holes will be drilled, separated by thin stringers. For these use strips of sapele about 32 mm (1 ¼ in.) wide cut cross grain. The longer these strips are cut the more boards can be made at once. Lay out the six strips with white stringers in between and tape them all together as shown in Fig. 138. Using a try-square, trim one end of the assembly square and then continue to cut strips about 20 mm (³/4 in) wide through the sapele and stringers. You need only two of the strips for each board.

You now have to construct a strip for the centre by a similar method using a series of strips and stringers to make it as colourful as possible. The centre of the construction shown in Fig. 139 used the off-cuts from the round cribbage board described later. The final

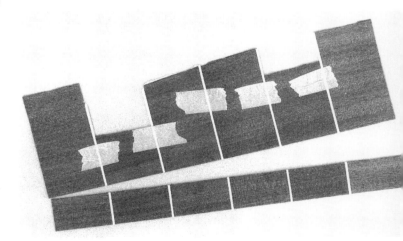

Fig. 138 Preparation of the playing area of the cribbage board, a band of six blocks

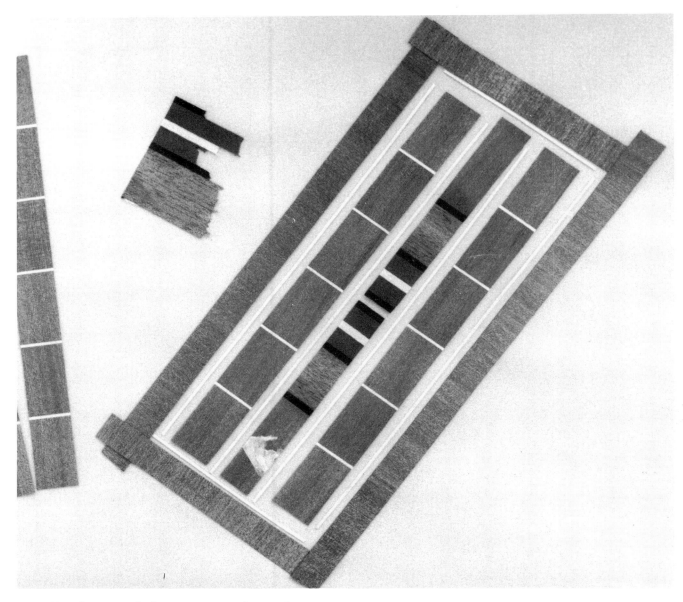

Fig. 139 The veneers laid out to construct the complete playing surface

width must be the same as the initial assembly so that the strip lengths are the same. Cut this into strips of about 25 mm (1 in.) to suit your preference. Now tape the three strips together with further white stringer separating them.

The playing area is now complete; check that the sides are straight and parallel and the ends square. Sapele borders can now be added which can be either cross or long grain with a white stringer inserted around the playing area. Cut the mitres as described in Chapter 7 (Cutting standard borders). The borders should be wide enough to allow mouldings to be cut round the edge if required.

Now lay the finished veneer assembly as detailed

in Chapter 7, preferably on to a solid piece of mahogany about 20 mm (³/4 in.) thick.

Our sample board shows that we moulded round the top edge of the board with a router. At this stage it is advisable to apply the sealer and build up several layers, being careful not to fill in the moulding, and rubbing down to a smooth finish.

Ten peg holes, made up of two rows of five, are required in each sapele oblong. This gives a total of 60 down each outer strip. Drill the holes on the pillar drill, setting up a fence for the two outside rows of holes and resetting for the inner rows. This ensures that the holes are in a straight line and is far more accurate than simply marking out; it is also much quicker. With a little practice the sets of five holes can be judged by eye, by first drilling the two end holes then the centre and finally spacing the two intermediate holes between those drilled. The inner rows are simply lined up with the outer. This method also saves rubbing down the surface again to remove marking out lines.

An extra hole at the centre of each end is also required for starting and finishing the game. Drill two holes in the end section of the mahogany to house the pins when not in use – large enough for the pins to fit in side by side.

The board can now have its final coat of sealer which is better applied from an aerosol can to prevent the holes and moulds filling up. The mouldings in particular are very difficult to polish by hand without causing a build-up of lacquer and obscuring the contours.

The final stage is to make a cover for the storage holes. We used a small strip of brass large enough to cover both holes, drilled and countersunk in the middle to act as a pivot on a brass screw.

ROUND CRIBBAGE BOARD (colour section)

To understand the design of the board it is necessary to appreciate the rudiments of the scoring system. When scoring on the oblong board you travel up and down your chosen side of the grid twice, finishing on the centre hole, giving a total of 121 pegged holes. On the round board you travel only once round the board which is divided into segments of five holes.

As a result 24 spear-like segments are required with five holes and one segment with one hole on which you start and finish ([24 × 5] + 1 = 121).

Method

1. You need a template to cut the segments accurately. A pattern is required first with an angle of 14.4° (360/25); even with an adjustable setsquare this is not too easy. To make a pattern, as illustrated in Fig. 140:
(a) draw a circle 300 mm (12 in.) in diameter;
(b) draw a 30° segment from the centre;
(c) bisect the angle to form a 15° segment;
(d) mark off 1.5 mm (¹⁄₁₆ in.) on the circumference and hence reduce the segment from this point to the centre.

This small reduction in the angle of every segment should add up to the one extra segment required.

Now transfer the paper pattern to a piece of plywood or aluminium to be cut and sanded down to size on the disc sander.

2. To prepare the veneer cut into various width parallel strips, a minimum of 500 mm (20 in.) long, and tape these together to form a block about 150 mm (6 in.) wide. In the demonstration sample the selected veneers were:

2 pieces cross-grained mahogany	38 mm (1¹⁄₂ in.) wide
4 pieces black stringers	3 mm (¹⁄₈ in.) wide
1 piece white stringer	3 mm (¹⁄₈ in.) wide
2 pieces long-grain mahogany	25 mm (1 in.) wide
2 pieces long-grain dyed red veneer	8 mm (⁵⁄₁₆ in.) wide

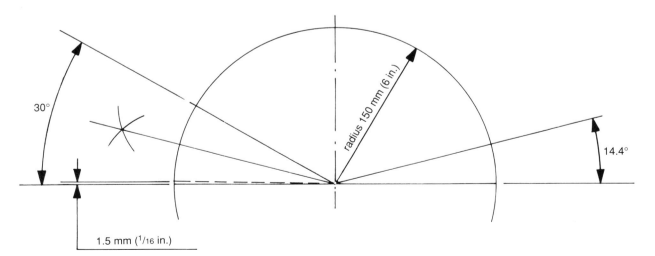

Fig. 140   Construction of segment for circular cribbage board pattern

These were made up into a pattern as shown in Fig. 141. Note that:

- the pattern is symmetrical about the centre white stringer so that the pattern is the same if cut from either side.
- the outside strip is the cross-grained veneer to prevent the points of the spears breaking away.
- the 25 mm (1 in.) wide strip is the one that the pin holes will be drilled into and hence should be towards the outer edge.

Build the strips up on several strips of masking tape secured, adhesive face up, on a suitable piece of board. When the pattern is complete use gummed tape to cover all the joints on what will become the face side. Now remove the masking tape – a worthwhile precaution is to run PVA adhesive into all the joints at this point and leave for about an hour or so to set.

3. You can now start to make your spears using

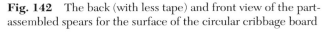

Fig. 141 A sample of the strips ready for taping together for the circular cribbage board and the spears cut from this assembly

Fig. 142 The back (with less tape) and front view of the part-assembled spears for the surface of the circular cribbage board

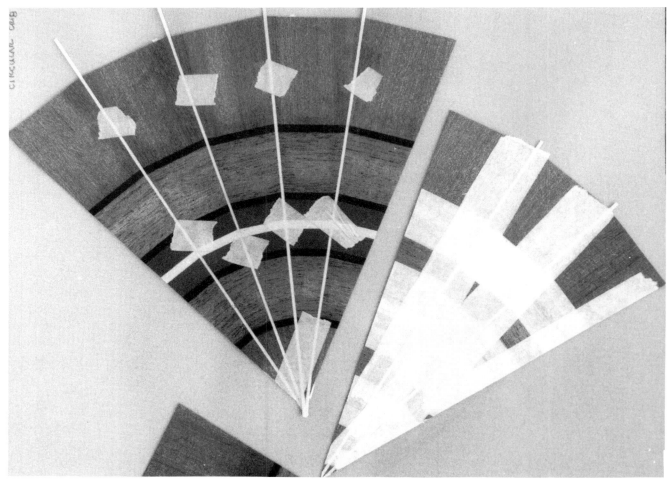

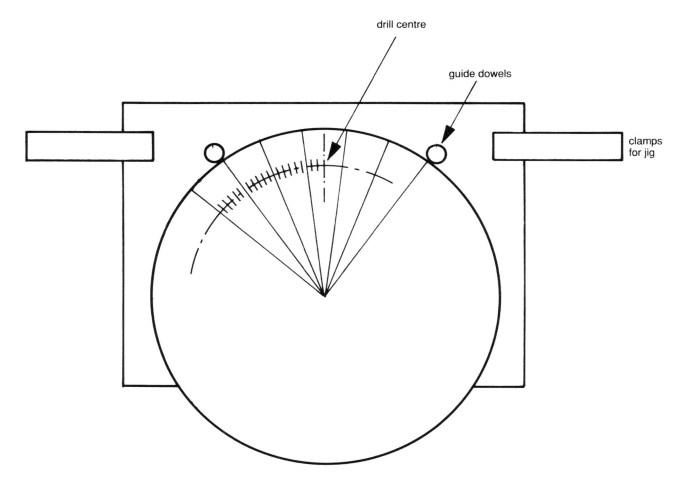

Fig. 143 Drill jig for circular components for round cribbage board

the template which you have made. Because the pattern is equal about the centre line we can cut the spears one up then one down, thus reducing the amount of waste veneer to a minimum.

4. When you have cut your 24 segments start taping them together with masking tape (Fig. 142), on the underside, with a white stringer between all adjacent segments to separate each grid. With the 24 segments in place you should be left with a space which in theory should be exactly the same as the other segments, but in practice there is likely to be a small difference. Fill this space with a plain veneer cut using the space in the taped-up assembly as a pattern to obtain an accurate fit.

5. Turn the face side up, fix all the joints again with gummed tape, remove the masking tape from the under side and smear PVA adhesive into joints.

6. Make a circle in MDF, using the home-made jig described in Chapter 5, to the size of your assembled veneer (about 300 mm, 12 in. in diameter).

7. After laying the veneer on the disc damp the gummed tape (don't flood it) and scrape it off before sanding flat.

8. If you wish to stain the edge of the board now is the time to apply a few coats of sealer. The edge can then have a fancy moulding cut with the router to take the sharpness off and the stain applied without danger of bleeding into the facing veneers.

9. Drill the peg holes, again using the pillar drill or stand-mounted electric drill, and using the jig as illustrated in Fig. 143. By revolving the disc against the two pegs all the holes can be drilled in a circle at a fixed distance from the edge. Two lines of holes are required with five holes in each patterned spear and one in the plain spear.

Before drilling holes in any boards of this type be sure that your drill bits are sharp, otherwise you will end up, at best, with a frayed edge to the hole or, at worst, with pieces of veneer chipped out between the holes which can be difficult to repair now that the sealer is applied.

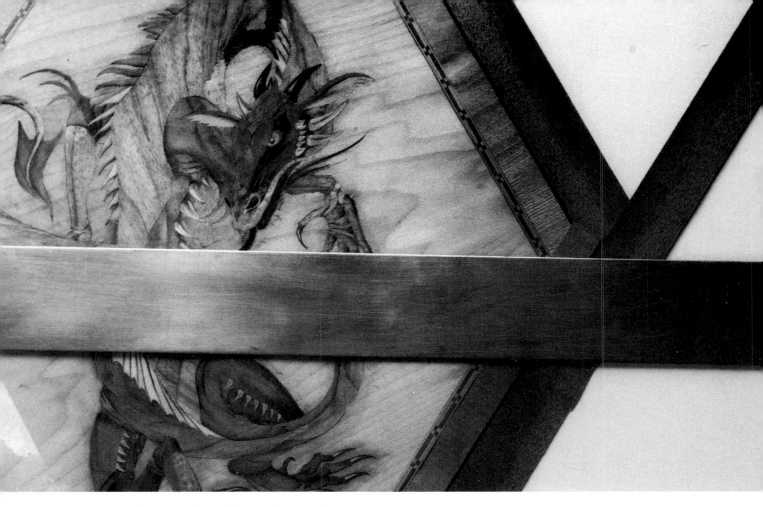

Fig. 144　Steel straight edge in place to aid cutting the mitres

Our board has a handling knob of turned mahogany in the middle, which is decorated with some fancy borders. This serves three purposes: to lift the board, to hide any slight faults at the centre junction and, as it is hollow, to house the scoring pegs when not in use. It also has four small feet which were turned on the lathe.

The finished board was given several coats of aerosol lacquer.

Fig. 145　View of the mitre ready for cutting

CHINESE CHECKERS

This project is described in the order in which it was carried out, but it is not crucial to follow this order exactly.

First we decided on a Chinese dragon as a design for the lid and chose a piece of Indian Silver Grey veneer for its body. This was unusual in having a suggestion of green in its background colour (this veneer tends to be pale yellow-brown with greyish grain markings) and also in having a well-defined curled grain marking. The tight curves were ideal to convey the curvature of the body and tail which is difficult to achieve when using straight-grain woods even by careful cutting in or sand shading. However, with about a quarter of the body still to complete, this figured veneer ran out and we finished it off using a piece of magnolia with a similar grain and figuring and not too much of a contrast in colour.

Having completed the marquetry for the picture on the top, it was necessary to design the box itself.

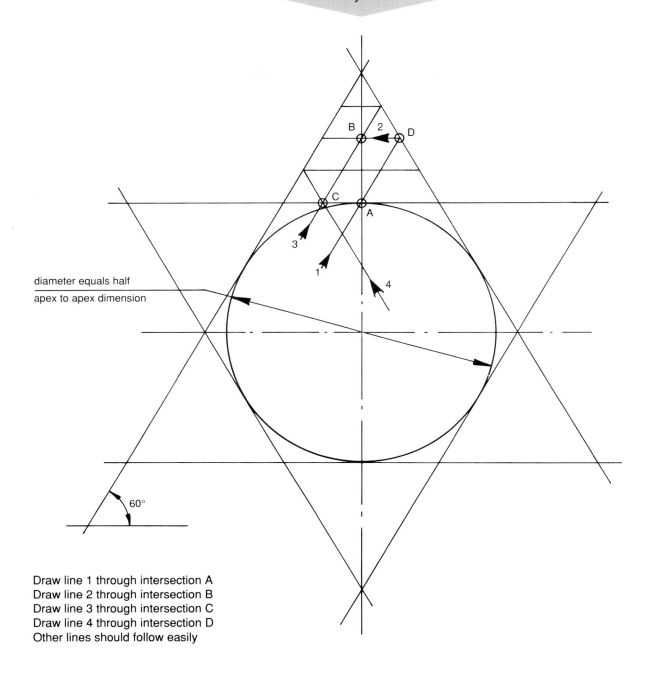

diameter equals half
apex to apex dimension

60°

Draw line 1 through intersection A
Draw line 2 through intersection B
Draw line 3 through intersection C
Draw line 4 through intersection D
Other lines should follow easily

Fig. 146 The geometric construction of the playing surface

As the playing surface is a six-pointed star we could have had a box which was rectangular, round or hexagonal. I had originally wanted a hexagonal design and fortunately this shape fitted in well with the position of the dragon on its waster.

An accurate, full-size drawing is required at this stage. For this you need a drawing board of A2 size or any suitable flat surface of this, or larger, size with one straight edge. A T square, 30–60 degrees set square and large pair of compasses are also required.

Having cut the design into a hexagon, prepare a border and tape it to the edges. The cutting of the

intersections at the corners is shown in Figs 144 and 145 and is the same technique as used for the picture-border mitres detailed in Chapter 7.

The lid and the games board were designed to be made from 15 mm (5/8 in.) MDF with the edges in a hardwood, probably mahogany, so that the edges could be shaped using a suitable router cutter, a bearing-guided Roman ogee. Working from the lid dimensions (putting the cart before the horse) the cross-section of the box can be determined and from this the size of the games area, which in turn defines the dimensions of the star.

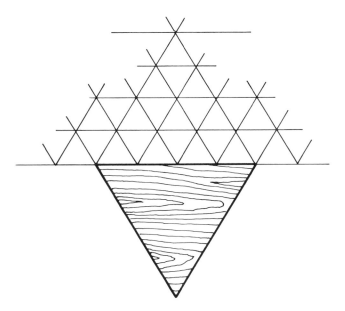

Fig 147 Large triangle removed and replaced with first contrast veneer

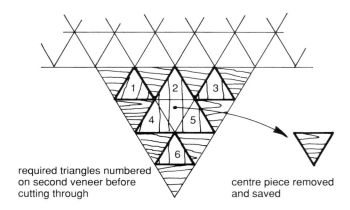

required triangles numbered on second veneer before cutting through

centre piece removed and saved

Fig. 148 Cutting of smaller triangles into large triangle and scored through into second contrast veneer

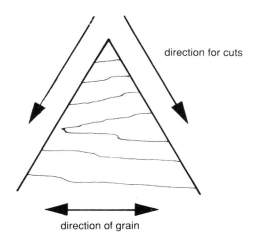

direction for cuts

direction of grain

Fig. 149 Avoiding broken tips to triangles

The construction of the play area requires only one dimension, drawing one circle, and careful use of the 30–60 degrees set square. Draw the circle with a diameter half the required distance across the corner of the star. Fig. 146 shows the sequence of construction. It is most important that it be accurate, and having produced the pattern on paper to get practice in the process of the geometrical construction we would advise you repeat it on the chosen waster (sycamore) by taping the veneer on the drawing board and accurately reconstructing the star. The usual process of using carbon paper to transfer the design leads to inaccuracy, and in the majority of cases this will show up badly in parquetry.

The small triangles could have been cut using a jig similar to that used for the Louis cubes, but in this case grain pattern of the veneers was maintained. Figs 147 and 148 show the way the first contrasting veneer is inset into the waster and the second veneer taped to the back and the cutting of the triangles achieved through the two layers. Lining up the rule with the original lines on the pattern gives accurate cutting and as the top veneer is removed the second sheet is numbered to ensure the triangles are set back into their correct position to maintain the grain pattern and ensure accurate fits. Note also that the direction of cutting at the tip of the triangle is important if you wish to retain the points (see Fig. 149).

Organizing dark veneers round the outside edge

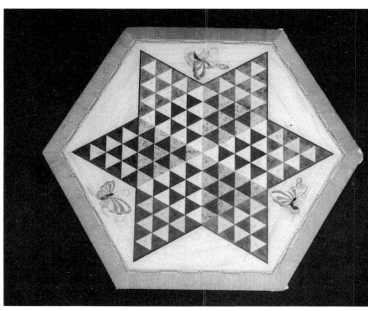

Fig. 150 Playing surface of the checkers board ready for glueing onto the base

120

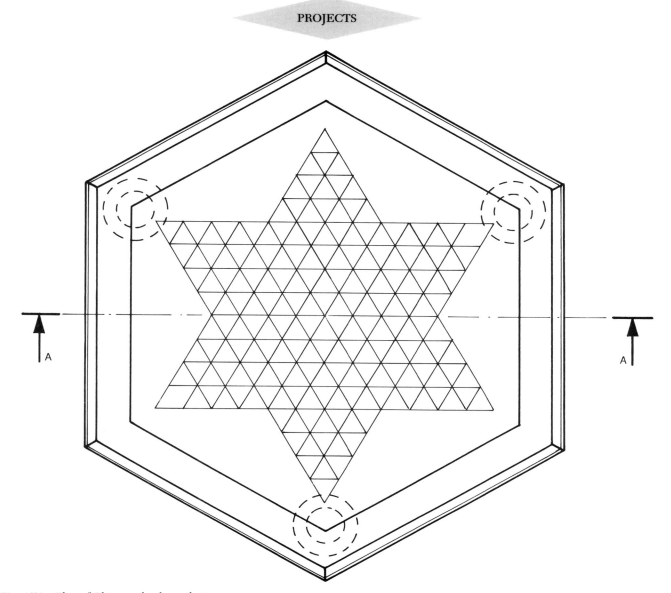

Fig. 151 Plan of Chinese checkers playing area

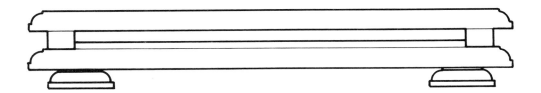

Fig. 152 Section A-A with cover in place

means that light veneers meet in the middle and hence some variation in light veneers is required. Fun can be had designing layouts of various light/dark veneers to see how many, or how few, different veneers are required. Fig. 150 shows a playing surface with ten veneers used in the layout.

To add a little more interest Chinese butterflies were added and to give more continuity with the lid, the borders on the lid were repeated on the playing surface. Figs 151–152 are drawings of the final design. Note that the playing area is slightly raised to locate the lid.

Fig. 153 Parquetry for the backgammon box lid

BACKGAMMON BOX

As can be seen from the part-completed lid in Fig. 153 and Fig. 47, p. 54) the design is made up of trellis and a parquetry panel consisting of two sets of radiating lines in each half of the design. The centre and corners could include any features representing the games board to be enclosed. In this case the layout of the counters on the board has been shown in the centre and the counters and dice in the corners. Chess would fit well into this design as would several other board games.

The marquetry on the inside of the box is relatively simple and the box itself was made up using the mitred method as detailed earlier in this chapter.

122

TURNED WORK

The particular nature of turned surfaces leaves little scope for large areas of applied marquetry, as we are restricted to applying our prepared panels of veneer to straight-sided cylinders. However, the flat surface on the lid of small jars, pill boxes and jewellery boxes makes an ideal place to decorate turned components, as is the base of plates, plaques and clocks.

PLATES, PLAQUES AND CIRCULAR CLOCKS

The circular plaque or plate clock can combine to good effect the basic skills of wood turning with the art of marquetry.

First turn the shallow plate, a typical section of which is shown in Fig. 154. When this is near completion, but not necessarily sanded or polished, turn out a shallow rebate with a scraping tool to a depth which is at least equal to, or preferably slightly deeper than, the thickness of the veneer.

As an essential aid cut a disc of MDF which is at least 12 mm (½ in.) thick, to the size of the finished picture or inlay. This will serve two purposes. It will be used to cut round the picture and also as a pattern when you cut the shallow recess in the bottom of the plate (Fig. 155). The disc must fit tightly into the recess and this will probably require the lathe being constantly turned on and off with many fittings as the recess is scraped gradually larger until a perfect fit is obtained. The bottom of the

recess must be perfectly flat or uneven pressure will result in blisters forming in the mounted veneer.

Cover the base of the recess in adhesive (PVA is suitable) and place the circular picture into the rebate. Cover in a sheet of plastic and several layers of paper. The disc is now used as a pressure plate: place it in position over the picture and clamp down with a series of G-cramps spaced not only round the edge of the disc but also toward the centre. Uneven pressure will result in blisters in the veneer which is difficult to repair, especially in the recessed plate (Fig. 156).

When you remove the pressure plate, after the glue has set, the surface of the veneer should be slightly lower than the turned surface of the plate, allowing you to sand down the plate to the required finish. The picture can also be cleaned up on the

Fig. 155 Prepared turned plate, marquetry circle and clamping disc ready for the assembly process

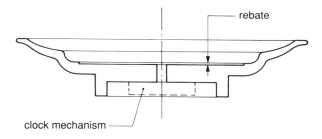

Fig. 154 Section through plate clock

rebate

clock mechanism

123

Fig. 156 Cramping the marquetry in the turned plate while the glue sets using the clamping disc

Fig. 157 Turned frame of the 'Toy Shop', stained but still with the centre of the disc attached. The frame is also polished in this state

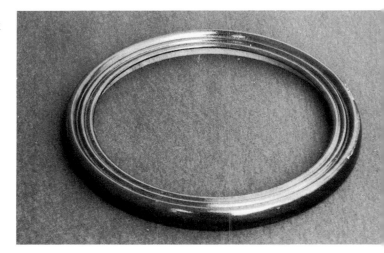

Fig. 158 Finished frame, polished and with the centre removed and the back recessed

revolving lathe, but take great care and turn off the lathe constantly to inspect the progress as the veneer can all too easily be sanded through.

The sealer, or whatever finish you are going to use, can also be applied safely on this lathe as the plate is rotated by hand, and then burnished to a very high gloss if required.

For clock variations of this plate, now drill a hole for the spindle through the middle of the face and fix the movement to the back.

The 'Toy Shop' as produced by a slightly different process. The frame was turned, a recess taken out of the back with the router and picture-mounted on a flat sheet on MDF. Both picture and frame were polished before assembly. The stages of making can be seen in Figs 157 to 159. As we have said before reflections from window glass are always difficult to reproduce in wood: study photographs of similar subjects before attempting something like this. Snow scenes also have their problems: the marquetry joints between light veneers often show up as dark lines, even when tightly cut. Therefore, avoid this type of picture unless you can construct the light area from single sheets of veneer.

Fig. 159 Marquetry for the 'Toy Shop' mounted onto MDF ready to cut into a disc to fit inside the frame

CYLINDRICAL SURFACES

We will concern ourselves mainly with the veneering round the circumference of fruit bowls and other similar shapes.

1. All the actual turning work must first be completed down to the sanding stage.

2. The surface to be veneered must be recessed to a depth of the thickness of the veneer to a perfect straight cylinder, a protruding veneer face giving rise to problems when you get to the sanding and cleaning up stage. It is always easier to bring the

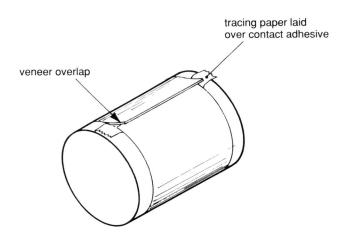

Fig. 160 Veneering a simple turned cylinder

surrounding wood down to the veneer rather than the other way round.

3. Now, with the aid of a paper or thin card template, determine the exact length of the veneer panel. For your first attempt it is advisable to cut the panel cross grain (the grain to run parallel to the axis of the cylinder) as this will prove more pliable and easier to bend round the cylinder. Cut it slightly longer than the circumference detemined and apply gummed tape to the top and bottom edges to prevent splitting.

4. Work out your design. In the case of the sweet jar (see colour section) we had five round pictures that had to be accurately spaced along the strip.

5. To fix your marquetry to the turned bowl use a contact adhesive. Apply it to both mating surfaces and leave for the recommended time. Before putting

Fig. 162   Recess for the veneer shown in profile

the veneer to the bowl place a narrow strip of tough paper (tracing paper is ideal) across the proposed beginning of the strip and lay the start of the veneer panel over this. Now lay the rest of the veneer panel, rubbing with a smooth flat object from the middle outwards to avoid trapping air and causing blisters. As the laying is completed the veneers will overlap (Fig. 160), probably more than you expected as the veneeer will stretch during rubbing down.

6. Lay a straight edge along the overlap and cut through both pieces of veneer. Remove the scraps of veneer and tracing paper and bring the ends together and rub them down to create, you hope, an invisible joint. The paper, as you will have observed, was to stop the veneer from sticking and avoid the

Fig. 161   Turned blank bowl ready for the application of the side veneer

Fig. 163   Application of the prepared veneer using a thermo-setting adhesive cured with a hot iron

Fig. 164   Base of the bowl still on its lathe face place

problem of having to chisel out the remains of the waste veneer and reglue the joints.

7. Before sanding on the lathe, remove any gummed paper by scraping or sanding lightly by hand using a block. When you use a lathe at speed to remove tape the sandpaper has a habit of sliding over the tape while sanding away the surrounding areas! If you want to do this take great care and stop at regular intervals to inspect the work for thinning veneer.

FRUIT BOWL

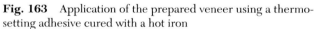

A typical application of this technique to produce a fruit bowl is shown in the series of photographs Figs. 161 to 164. In this example the veneer was applied with a thermo-setting adhesive which was

set with a hot iron. The centre of the bowl was turned out after the exterior was finished, to maintain stability during the veneering and veneer finishing operations.

WEED POT (Fig. 165)

Another popular and interesting way to decorate turned items of this sort is to use parquetry designs. A small band of Louis cubes has been used on the small vase or 'weed pot'; as it is sometimes called. This creates a problem where the ends of the panel meet as you cannot cut the joint straight across the cube pattern without this being very noticeable. To overcome this the mating ends must resemble a piece of jigsaw puzzle and be cut along the joint

Fig. 165   Use of the Louis cube design on a weed pot

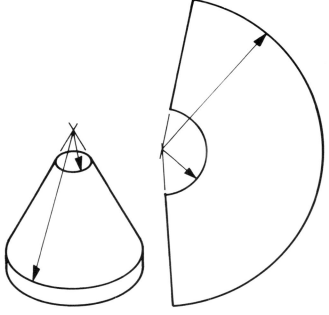

Fig. 167   Pattern for conical shape

lines of the pattern (see Fig. 166). This requires a reverse technique:

1. The Louis cube band is completed first, the length equalling the required circumference of the pot (see Fig. 43, p. 53).

2. A pattern is made, including the staggered joint, from paper, thin card or veneer.

3. The wood is now turned, checking frequently, until the pattern joins perfectly when wrapped round. As a perfect fit may prove impossible it is advantageous to have a slight overlap as it is easier to trim the pattern lightly than try to add small pieces to the edges of the diamonds. A small difference is very hard to detect in an intricate pattern like this.

OTHER SHAPES

True conical shapes present no real problems provided you first make a template with which to cut your veneer (Fig. 167). Due to the tight bend at the top it may be wise to arrange the veneers with the grain toward the apex (circular crib board fashion). This will also hide the join line.

A globe or spherical shape proves much more difficult and will require the pieces of veneer to be cut and glued individually (maybe using the male/female clamp method as for the domed clock) as the pattern progresses.

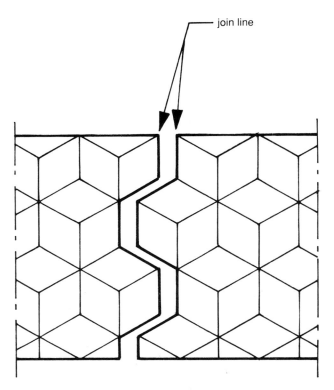

join line

Fig. 166   Join line when louis cube design wrapped round cylinder

128

LARGE FLAT SURFACES

The laying of large areas of marquetry can be difficult and the subsequent problems with sanding flat and finishing increase in proportion to the area. Time is also a factor when attempting large areas of marquetry and the possibility of rubbing through the veneer tends to increase as mechanical means are employed to prepare the veneers for polishing in a reasonable time. As a result it is rare for the amateur marquetarian to attempt areas of much more than 350 × 450 mm (14 × 18 in.).

In the main large areas are usually covered in plain veneer using consecutive leaves to repeat the pattern on the long axis of four quartered as described in Chapter 6. The amount of marquetry tends to be small, the beauty of the wood being sufficient to please the eye.

The advantage of veneering large areas is that the modern backing material used (MDF) is very stable, is available in large sheets (unlike solid timber which must be jointed), is cheap relative to good quality hardwood and is environmentally friendly, using only a fraction of the amount of hardwood used in solid furniture.

TABLE TOP (colour section)

The shape of this table top required a quartered veneer. In this case the four-quartered pieces were consecutive leaves of maple burr cut to give a radiating effect from the centre. The effect was so good it was tempting to forgo any further marquetry.

The background pattern of the centre design is ideal for cutting with the saw if available, but in this case the window method was used. As many joins must be made in the curling pattern great care must be taken to ensure that the grain follows in the same direction. The joins are difficult to hide in light veneers and impossible if the grain flow changes direction. A little sand shading was used to give an impression of depth as the background pattern disappeared behind the peonies. Zig-zag cutting was used on the flower petals as a means of colour graduation without hard lines.

No attempt was made to add a hardwood edge as it would have been impossible to match the face veneer. After cutting to shape, balancing veneers were applied to both sides. Because of the area a contact adhesive was used. The face and a further balancing veneer were applied, again with contact adhesive. After sanding flat and applying several coats of polish the edges were moulded, sanded, and a stain applied to match the face. This process prevented the stain leaching into the face veneer.

The top was finished in an acid-catalysed lacquer to give it a surface resistant to hot coffee cups, but care was taken not to fill the moulded edge.

CABINET DOORS (colour section)

Already part of a pleasant television cabinet veneered in sapele, inlaid with curl mahogany, this pair of doors had the largest area of any project in this book. We decided to liven them up with some marquetry. Madrona burr seemed to complement the reddish-brown colour of the sapele so two four-quartered panels were made up as described in Chapter 6. These were further endowed with white stringers, cross-grain sapele banding around the edge and broken corners which can be seen in Figs 56 (p. 60) and 57 (p. 60)

A motif of Chinese latticework and chrysanthemums was chosen to form the centrepiece (125 mm, 5 in. diameter) of each door, made as a matching pair. The veneers used were Swiss pear for the background, makore for the lattice work, and sapele, pear and sycamore to form the flower petals in which the spear joining method was used as described in Chapter 5. The thin lines around the edge of the leaf scrolls were obtained by cutting makore into the entire area of the leaf, leaving this until the PVA adhesive had dried, and then cutting in the sycamore leaving just a thin line of makore round the edge.

Two circular templates were cut on the disc sander for cutting the design and the hole in the centre of each panel.

A thin hardwood lipping was mitred and glued all round the edges of the doors, and when dry was scraped and sanded level with the MDF used for the bulk of the doors. Make sure there is no slight bevel at the edge as this will prevent even pressure being applied up to the edges.

Laying these panels was always going to be the biggest problem because of their size. The easiest method for those of you without a press would be to use a contact adhesive. Our largest press was 400 × 350 mm (16 × 14 in.), and our doors were 610 × 310 mm (24$^{1}/_{2}$ × 12$^{1}/_{2}$ in.). The problem was overcome by using two spare sheets of MDF larger than the doors as pressure plates. The doors were pressed, one at a time, using Cascamite as the adhesive. When glued and laid in between polythene sheets and paper the door was placed between the two sheets of MDF and the whole sandwich cramped in the press. The overhanging boards were cramped together with G-cramps. This system worked perfectly.

When sanded and cleaned up ready for polishing they first received a coat of mahogany-coloured wood filler. This is a muddy paste which is wiped on and off quickly to fill the grain and to try to match the colour with the rest of the cabinet. Do not use this unless absolutely necessary as it can take the sharpness out of the marquetry. The doors were finished in an acid-catalysed lacquer.

ODDMENTS

In this section we include some small items which require relatively little woodworking equipment.

LETTER RACK

The idea for this project was taken from a similar item seen in a gift shop with shaped front, back and sides added for extra interest. The low cut out at the front was included as a practical touch, to enable small items in the front section to be visible.

The first task was to decide on the construction of the letter rack and a drawing was produced as shown in Fig. 168. From this design the area available for marquetry was determined and a pattern drawn. To give a wrap-around effect the front and ends were designed, and the marquetry carried out, in one long strip. (At this stage make sure that you have sufficient veneer from a single sheet, or matching leaves, to cover all surfaces of the board used, back and front.)

The border bands were cut first, but on reflection we would recommend that the stringers be slightly thinner than in the example illustrated. After careful drawing of the circle and semi-circles direct on to the veneer they were all cut by hand. Here again it would be better to use the template method as described in Chapter 5.

Sand shading on leaves and petals is always going to give a more realistic and pleasing effect than the plain, flat effect that is produced if you use untreated veneeers. The centres of the flowers were produced by the fragmentation process. Fig. 169 shows the marquetry in a part-complete stage.

All the vertical pieces were made from 5 mm (¹/4 in.) thick MDF which if veneered on both sides is the material least likely to warp. Great care must be taken when cutting the board to size. Cut the straight edges on a fine-tooth circular saw and the curves with a hand fretsaw, although a mechanical fretsaw or Vibro saw would be ideal if you have one.

Order of manufacture
1. Cut all the top edges, those which have to be veneered, to size, remembering that a thickness of veneer is to be added and hence the finished size should be about 0.55 mm (¹/64 in.) inside the

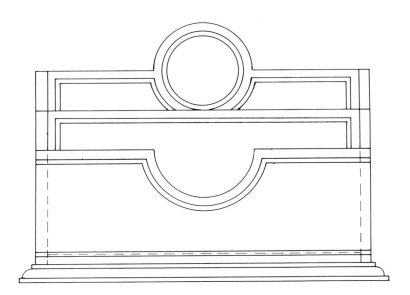

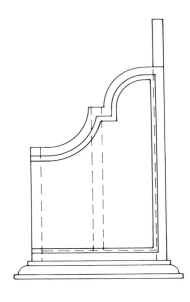

Fig. 168 Design for the letter rack

Fig. 169 Marquetry for the letter rack in progress

required size. The radii may need finishing off with a file to ensure smooth curves. The corner joints and base can be left oversize.

2. Then apply the top edge veneers, cutting the veneer long grain for the straight edges and cross grain for the curves to make bending easier. Apply with a contact adhesive.

3. Next apply the inner and outer face veneers. Make sure that the top edges of the prepared marquetry align correctly with the cut board; masking tape may be needed to prevent slip occurring. In this case PVA adhesive is ideal for veneer application.

4. Having veneered all the faces, cut the bottom edge to size.

5. The corner joints are a simple glued mitre and are best formed on a sanding disc which is less likely to damage the facing veneers than by cutting.

6. Cut grooves, the depth of the veneer, on the inside face of the end panels to locate the centre divider. Also, cut the centre divider to length.

7. Tape the corner joints to determine accurately the dimensions of the base. The base is best made from solid wood which if possible should match the facing veneer. It is difficult to see any way of producing this part other than with a router.

8. Having checked the parts will assemble correctly, sand down, seal and polish all surfaces. To polish after assembly would be impossible.

9. Gluing together is a simple task, using the masking tape hinge and PVA adhesive as was used on the jewellery box corners. The base can be held with masking tape; the centre divider should need no restraint.

10. To cover any small blemishes apply a cellulose spray finish after assembly.

Fig. 170 Zig-zag cutting applied to the petals on the dressing table mirror base

DRESSING-TABLE MIRROR

The basic design for the marquetry on the top of the base was adapted to fit the shape of the top, leaves and stems being bent to suit the curve of the sides and generally manipulated to fit the shape of the top as well as being 'mirror reflected' to make the design symmetrical about the centre. The finished marquetry can be seen in Fig. 170.

The veneers were applied to the sides and drawer front as described in Chapter 7 and illustrated in Fig. 84 (p. 75). The wasters and constructional wood were all mahogany enabling us to mould all the edges lavishly with the router. The two mirror supports were turned on the lathe.

The marquetry technique involved in the petal construction is explained Chapter 5. The completed article was finished using a semi-matt cellulose aerosol spray to avoid losing the detail in the mouldings.

KEY TIDY

A simple way of turning a piece of marquetry into applied marquetry.

This little bullfinch was redrawn from a Christmas card and again zig-zag cutting was used to blend in the variations of colour on the breast which can be seen in Fig. 171. The letters, being cut from the back, must be reversed by simply turning the tracing paper over after drawing or tracing.

The mounting board is 12 mm ($\frac{1}{2}$ in.) MDF and after the facing veneer was mounted on the shaped board a moulded edge was produced with the router.

TABLE-LAMP BASE

A deceptively simple-looking project. The waster of the butterfly and blackberry design was selected to

Fig. 171 Detail from the key tidy, illustrating the use of zig-zag cutting to produce a feather effect

Fig. 172 Completed key tidy

Fig. 174 Table lamp base

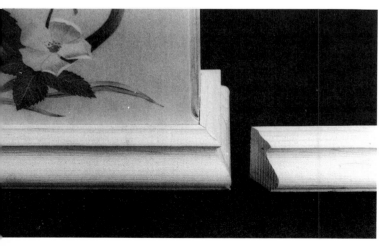

Fig. 173 Moulding for the table lamp base

match, as near as possible, the timber from which the body would be made.

The small turned top is not a separate piece but turned from the main block. After rough shaping the block on a band saw, the round top and shoulder were turned. With this shape of wood the turning operation can be very dangerous and should only be undertaken by experienced woodturners. A simple alternative would be to turn the top cylinder and shape the main block with the band saw, gluing the two together just before the spray finish is applied.

The hard edge is removed with a moulding using the router and the base was created from a softwood moulding as can be seen in Fig. 174.

APPENDIX

PLANS FOR MARQUETRY DESIGNS

The designs on the following pages are taken from some of the projects in the book and will help get you started. They can be used on, or adapted for, any number of items.

PARQUETRY DESIGN (p. 136 and cover)

We produced this design specially for the cover of this book, but it could be used for any small horizontal surface. The frames of the squares/diamonds were made from home-made bandings, but commercial bandings could be used, constructed on a separate waster. The trellis can be cut into a quartered burr for ease of cutting and background interest. The diamonds can then be cut into the trellis using the reverse window method.

GAMES BOX LID (p. 137)

This design could be adapted for the lid of any board game. The parquetry is best cut using the window method after transferring the design straight onto the waster. The radiating squares should be cut in contrasting veneer with the grain radiating out from the centre of construction. Designs for the playing pieces can be included in the corner circles and the board in the centre ellipse.

BAMBOO DESIGN (p. 138)

A design for the inverted 'U' clock. The leaves are cut from magnolia and light green stained veneer. Each half section of leaf is sand scorched before assembly. The bamboo poles can be made of any yellowish veneer and lightly sand scorched along one edge. This design is best used on a dark background such as walnut.

CHRYSANTHEMUM ROSETTE (p. 139)

This design was used on the ends of the tea caddy and in an enlarged version on the cabinet doors. All the pieces require double cutting: first cut in all the pieces in a dark outline veneer, then cut the window for the specimen veneer, leaving a thin line of the black, 0.8 mm ($^1/_{32}$ in.) if possible. Take great care and leave the black pieces to dry before undertaking any further work.

THIRD AND GOAL (p. 140)

This three-veneer picture was adapted from a black and white picture taken from a newspaper. Sycamore was used in the background (waster), and a leaf each of American and European walnut was ideal for the figures, because of the tonal range available in a single sheet.

CHAPLIN CLOCK DESIGN (p. 141)

This design was used on the inverted 'U' clock, but could easily be adapted for any flat surface. If used on a clock the sky/waster should match the rest of the clock. Aspen will create pale flesh tones, and dyed black veneer can be used for the hat, jacket and moustache.

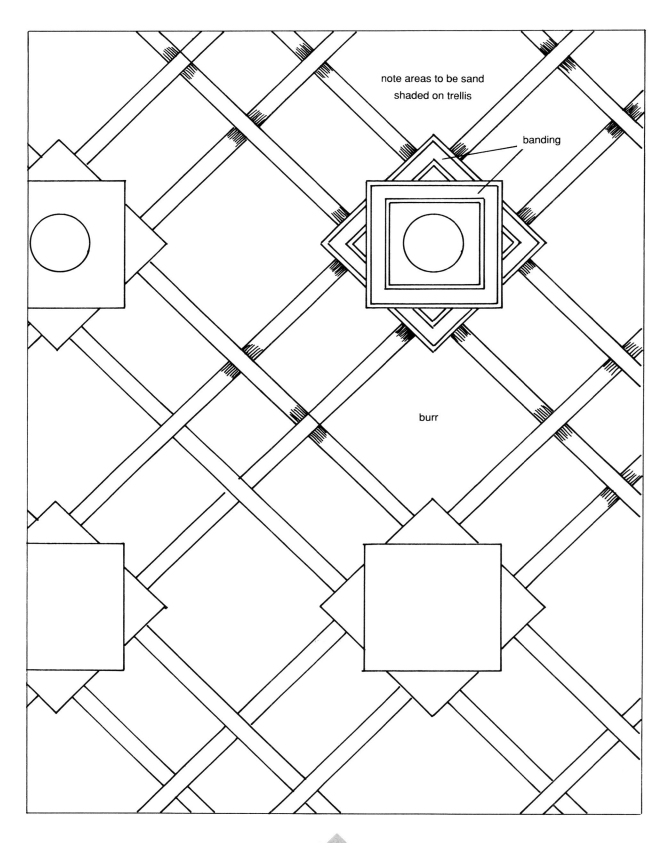

note areas to be sand
shaded on trellis

banding

burr

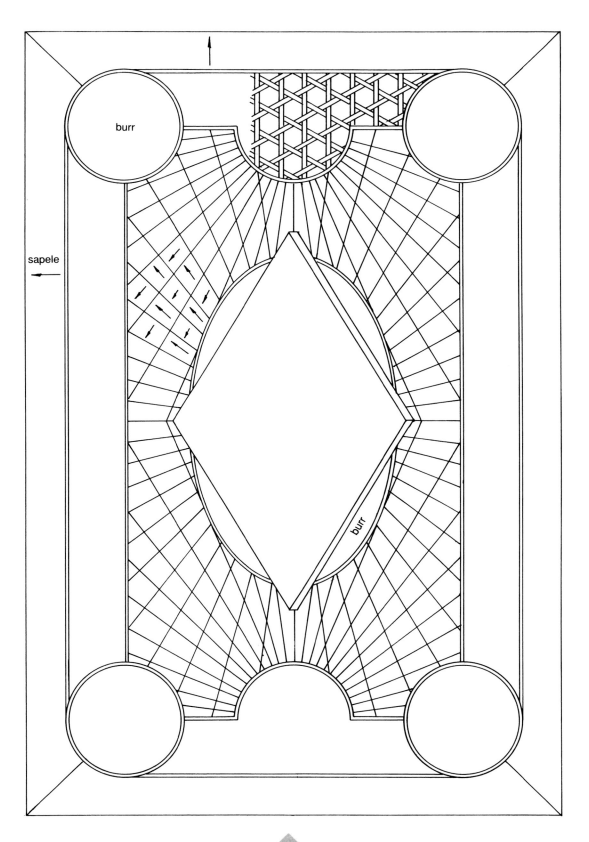

burr

sapele

burr

position of hole for quartz movement

note areas of sand scorching on leaves and bamboo cane

direction of grain

138

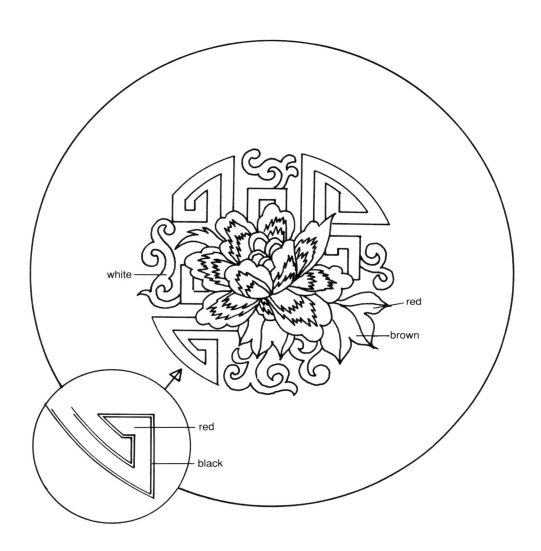

140

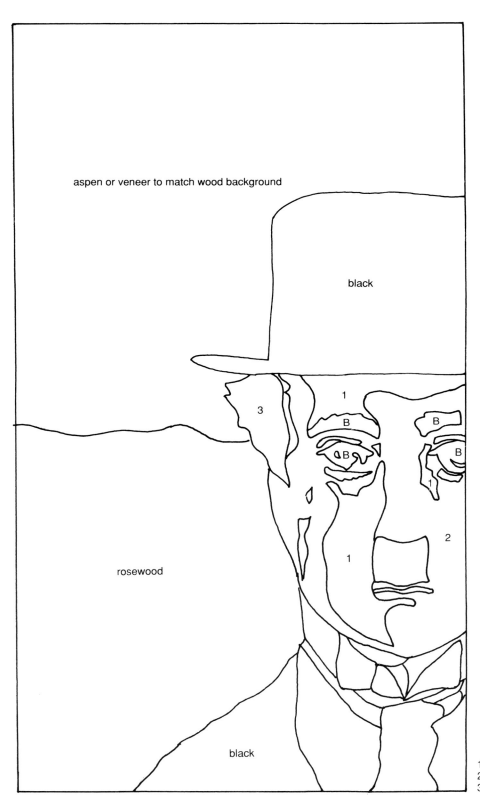

aspen or veneer to match wood background

black

3

1

B

B

B

B

1

rosewood

1

2

black

1 sap walnut
2 horse chestnut
3 walnut burr

LIST OF SUPPLIERS

Suppliers of veneers

U.K.

Art Veneers,
Chiswick Ave.,
Industrial Estate,
Mildenhall,
Suffolk, IP28 7AY

Fine Veneers,
75 Windsor Ave.,
Hillingdon,
Middx., UB10 9AU

Abbey Marquetry,
Unit 14,
Fiddlebridge Industrial Unit,
Lemsford Road,
Hatfield,
Herts., AL10 0DE

John Boddy Timber Ltd.,
Riverside Sawmills,
Boroughbridge,
North Yorks., YO5 9LJ

Alan Holtham,
Old Stores Turnery,
Wistaston Road,
Willaston,
Nantwich,
Cheshire, CW5 6QJ

J. Crispen & Sons,
92–96 Curtain Road,
London, EC2

Furness Craftwoods,
Vally Farm Barn,
Golden Lane,
Thorpe-le-Soken,
Essex, CO16 0LE

R. Aaronson Veneers Ltd.,
45 Redchurch Street,
London, E2

U.S.A.

Artistry in Veneers Ltd.,
450 Oak Tree Ave.,
Plainfield,
N.J. 07080

B. & B. Rare Woods,
10946 W. Texas Ave.,
Lakeland Co., 80232

Certainly Woods,
11753 Big Tree Road,
RT 20A East Aurora,
N.Y. 14052

Albert Constantine & Son Inc.,
2050 East Chester Road,
Bronx,
N.Y. 10461

Woodshed, 1807 Elmwood Ave.,
Buffalo,
N.Y. 14207

Suppliers of clock movements etc.

Tudor Craft,
Unit 12,
Titan Way,
Britannia Enterprise Park,
Lichfield,
Staffs., WS14 9TT

C. & L. Clocks,
Kings Hill Industrial Estate,
Bude,
Cornwall

Finishing materials

J. W. Bollom & Co.,
P.O. Box 78,
Beckenham,
Kent, BR3 4BL

Rustins Ltd.,
Waterloo Road,
London, NW2 7TX

FURTHER INFORMATION

FURTHER READING

M. Campkin, *The Technique of Marquetry*, Batsford 1988

H.J. Hobbs & H.E. Fitchett (eds), *Marquetry Society of America's Modern Marquetry Handbook*, Thames and Hudson 1978

A. Jackson & D. Day, *The Good Wood Handbook*, Harper Collins 1991

W.A. Lincoln, *The Complete Manual of Wood Veneering*, Stobart Davies 1984

W.A. Lincoln, *The Marquetry Manual*, Stobart Davies 1989

W.A. Lincoln, *World Woods in Colour*, Stobart Davies 1986

N. Lofthouse, *The Woodworker's Pocket Palette*, Batsford 1993

The Marquetry Society, *The Marquetarian*, quarterly

Pierre Ramond, *Marquetry*, Taunton Press, USA 1989

F. Oughton, *The Craft Manual of Wood Finishing*, Stobart Davies 1986

Aidan Walker, *Wood Polishing and Finishing Techniques*, Ebury Press 1985

VIDEO

Ernie Ives, *Marquetry for Beginners*, Breakaway Tackle Film Production (available from The Marquetry Society of Great Britain, address below)

USEFUL ADDRESSES

Note: these may change as officers of the societies change, but will still serve as a point of first contact.

The Marquetry Society of Great Britain
Magazine Editor (*The Marquetarian*)
Ernie Ives
63 Church Lane,
Sproughton,
Ipswich,
Suffolk, IP8 3AY

Marquetry Society of America
P.O. Box 224
Lindenhurst,
New York, 11757
U.S.A.

Marquetry Society of Ontario
Mike Stradwick
6 Pinedale Court,
Kitchener,
Ontario N2E 1KG
Canada

The Marquetry Society of Victoria, Australia
Roy Turner
30 Clan Brae Ave.,
Burwood,
Victoria, 3125
Australia

International Creative Marquetry Society
P.O. Box 396
Louisville,
Colorado 80027-0396
U.S.A.

INDEX